20th Century Drawings FROM THE WHITNEY MUSEUM OF AMERICAN ART

EXHIBITION ITINERARY

National Gallery of Art, Washington, D.C.
May 21–September 7, 1987

The Cleveland Museum of Art
September 30–November 8, 1987

Achenbach Foundation, California Palace of the
Legion of Honor, San Francisco
March 5–June 5, 1988

Arkansas Arts Center, Little Rock
June 30–August 28, 1988

Whitney Museum of American Art, Fairfield County, Stamford, Connecticut
November 17, 1988–January 25, 1989

This publication was organized at the Whitney Museum of American Art by Doris Palca, Head, Publications and Sales; Sheila Schwartz, Editor; and Vicki Drake, Secretary/Assistant.

The photography was coordinated by Anita Duquette, Manager, Rights and Reproductions, and Diana Wasserman, Secretary/Assistant.

Photograph Credits:
All black-and-white photographs are by Geoffrey Clements. All color photographs are by Gamma One Conversions, Inc., with the exception of Charles Burchfield, *Golden Dream*, photograph © 1985 by D. James Dee.

Designed by Elizabeth Finger.
Typeset by Craftsman Type Inc.
Printed in Hong Kong by the South China Printing Company.

Cover: David Smith, *Eng No. 6*, 1952
(see page 95).

Library of Congress Cataloging-in-Publication Data

Whitney Museum of American Art.
   20th-century drawings from the Whitney Museum of American Art.

   Bibliography: p.
   1. Drawing, American—Exhibitions. 2. Drawing, Modern—20th century—United States—Exhibitions. 3. Whitney Museum of American Art—Exhibitions. I. Cummings, Paul. II. Title. III. Title: Twentieth-century drawings from the Whitney Museum of American Art.
   NC108.W47 1987   741.973'074'01471   87-6112
ISBN 0-87427-053-7 (paper)
ISBN 0-393-02483-0 (cloth)

Copyright © 1987
Whitney Museum of American Art
945 Madison Avenue
New York, New York 10021

20th Century Drawings

FROM THE WHITNEY MUSEUM OF AMERICAN ART

PAUL CUMMINGS

Whitney Museum of American Art, New York

in association with W. W. Norton & Company, New York, London

Foreword

This catalogue and the accompanying exhibition represent milestones in the history of the Whitney Museum of American Art. Drawings had been of interest to the Museum since it was founded by Gertrude Vanderbilt Whitney in 1930, but a concentrated effort to assemble an outstanding collection had never been a priority. We now recognize drawings not as a secondary form of artistic expression, but as primary aesthetic statements, essential to the understanding of an artist's creative process. For this reason, it was decided in 1977 that it would be appropriate for the Whitney Museum to devote considerable attention and resources to developing the finest public collection of twentieth-century American drawings. Jules Prown, Paul Mellon Professor of the History of Art at Yale University and Trustee of the Whitney Museum, agreed to assist us by becoming the chairman of the first Drawing Committee to be organized at the Museum. A group of connoisseurs and patrons formed the Committee, and their work began and continues under the guidance of Paul Cummings, Adjunct Curator, Drawings.

Almost fifty percent of the works in this exhibition have been acquired in the last ten years through the efforts of the Drawing Committee. As a measure of our admiration and respect, the staff of the Whitney Museum and I dedicate this exhibition to the members of the Committee, whose support and generosity are responsible for much of what we accomplish.

Since the formation of the Drawing Committee, the Museum has assembled what can now be considered among the most comprehensive public collections of twentieth-century American drawings. We are proud of the quality of our holdings in this medium and very pleased to be able to share them with a wide public through this exhibition and catalogue. We are grateful to the institutions who have invited us to exhibit our collection and thus extend our enthusiasm for American graphic art across the nation.

None of our work would have been possible without the endorsement of the Trustees of the Whitney Museum and the cooperation and generous support of patrons, whose donations of drawings or purchase funds are gratefully acknowledged in the credit lines of each work.

We hope that through this catalogue and exhibition you will become more familiar with our dedication to quality in American art, particularly in the work of living artists, and will enjoy and appreciate the graphic achievements of those we consider to be among the finest artists of the century.

TOM ARMSTRONG
Director

Acknowledgments

This selection of master drawings from the Permanent Collection of the Whitney Museum of American Art was acquired through the good will and support of numerous people, many of whom are acknowledged in the credit lines of individual drawings. It is only through the continued interest of such patrons that this collection has been developed to its present size.

The works in the exhibition, which reviews most of the major schools from the turn of the century to the present, were chosen to demonstrate the place of the master drawing concept in twentieth-century American art. A master drawing is achieved when the artist combines imagination, idea, feeling, and technical accomplishment in a unity which exemplifies the highest attainments of that artist's style. Allowing for differences in time, culture, and styles, such drawings should compare favorably with those historical pages that have long received similar appellations.

Among the many individuals who have aided significantly in the development of this collection, I should like to acknowledge the encouragement of Howard Lipman, Leonard Lauder, and Tom Armstrong, the Museum's director, whose commitment to drawing has made both the collection and this exhibition possible. A special note of gratitude to Dr. Jules D. Prown, who has been the chairman of the Drawing Committee since its inception, conducting its proceedings with understanding and openmindedness; and to the other members of the Drawing Committee who have supported its activities with intelligent sophistication as well as through patronage and gifts of works of art.

Stephanie Schoch, my assistant, ably researched and compiled the bibliographies and exhibition histories, with assistance from Cheryl Epstein.

I am especially grateful to the directors, curators, and staffs of the participating museums for their support in presenting this exhibition.

PAUL CUMMINGS
Adjunct Curator, Drawings

Artists

Catalogue

Dimensions are in inches, followed by centimeters; height precedes width. Sight refers to measurements taken within the frame or mat opening. The accession number of a work refers to the year of acquisition and, after a decimal point, to the sequence of its addition to the Permanent Collection during that year. For example, 77.3 means the work was the third work acquired in 1977. Promised gifts are noted with the letter P and the order of the two figures is reversed.

If no provenance is provided, ownership could not be traced beyond the donor who gave the work to the Museum. The exhibition histories for each drawing only include exhibitions held after the work was acquired by the Whitney Museum. Full references to the Whitney Museum exhibition publications abbreviated in these histories are as follows:

WMAA 1978: *20th-Century American Drawings: Five Years of Acquisitions*, July 28–October 1, 1978. Catalogue by Paul Cummings.

WMAA 1979: *Twentieth-Century Drawings from the Whitney Museum of American Art: A Travel Exhibition*, 1979–81. Organized for travel. Brochure.

WMAA 1981: *Drawing Acquisitions 1978–1981*, September 17–November 15, 1981. Catalogue by Paul Cummings.

WMAA 1981a: Whitney Museum of American Art, Fairfield County, *Drawing Acquisitions 1978–1981*, December 18, 1981–February 3, 1982. Brochure.

WMAA 1982: *Abstract Drawings 1911–1981: Selections from the Permanent Collection*, May 5–July 11, 1982. Brochure.

WMAA 1983: *The Sculptor as Draftsman: Selections from the Permanent Collection*, September 15–November 13, 1983. Brochure.

WMAA 1984: *Sculptors' Drawings 1910–1980: Selections from the Permanent Collection*, 1984–85. Organized for travel. Brochure.

WMAA 1985: *Drawing Acquisitions 1981–1985*, June 11–September 22, 1985. Catalogue by Paul Cummings.

WMAA 1986: Whitney Museum of American Art at Philip Morris, *The Changing Likeness: Twentieth-Century Portrait Drawings: Selections from the Permanent Collection of the Whitney Museum of American Art*, June 27–September 3, 1986. Brochure.

Maurice Prendergast

1859–1924

Central Park, 1901, 1901
Watercolor on paper, 14⅜ x 21½
(36.5 x 54.6)
Purchase   32.42

PROVENANCE
The artist

EXHIBITIONS
Addison Gallery, Phillips Academy, Andover, Massachusetts, *The Prendergasts*, 1938; Walker Art Center, Minneapolis, *Exhibition of American Watercolorists Selected by Lloyd Goodrich*, 1945 (traveled); Albertina, Vienna, 1949; The Museum of Modern Art, New York, *Seven American Watercolorists*, 1953 (traveled); Wadsworth Atheneum, Hartford, *Off for the Holidays*, 1955; Museum of Fine Arts, Boston, *Maurice Prendergast Exhibition*, 1961 (traveled); Katonah Gallery, New York, *Maurice Prendergast Exhibition*, 1962; Santa Barbara Museum of Art, California, *Painted Paper: Watercolors from Dürer to Our Time*, 1962; Whitney Museum of American Art, New York, *Art of the United States: 1670–1966*, 1966, p. 153; Whitney Museum of American Art, *70 Years of American Art*, 1969; The Lowe Art Museum, University of Miami, Coral Gables, Florida, *French Impressionists Influence American Artists*, 1971; Whitney Museum of American Art, *The 20th Century: 35 American Artists*, 1974; Phoenix Art Museum, Arizona, *American Painting 1900 to 1932 from the Whitney Museum of American Art*, 1975, n.p. (traveled); Whitney Museum of American Art, *The Whitney Studio Club and American Art: 1900–1932*, 1975, p. 23; Whitney Museum of American Art, *American Painting 1900–1940*, 1976, n.p. (traveled);

Maurice Prendergast is often singled out as a pioneer of modernism in America. This reputation is founded on his stylistic relationship with European art, but Prendergast may have first experienced Eastern art, for in his native Boston Ernest Fenollosa, the philosopher and historian of Oriental culture, exerted an influence on Boston society toward the end of the nineteenth century. The atmosphere of the Orient clings to many Boston collections and is evident in the designs employed by the city's artists.

Prendergast was an artist who approached abstraction but never took the final step, possibly because the European ideas which spawned it were never supported by a broad, sophisticated segment of Boston culture. By reducing figures to nearly flat shapes, eliminating facial expression, pressing the depth required in depicting actuality into a two-dimensional pattern, he produced dense but representational compositions, whose color manipulations activate what could easily become a tapestry design.

Prendergast's watercolors present a world based on observation but transformed into one of elegance, removed from a realistic depiction of life about him. The silhouettes fit into the adjoining shapes like a jigsaw puzzle and the overall effect is like that of a Byzantine mosaic. Light falls evenly across the images. A luminous atmosphere fills the space with the joyfulness of a relaxed sunny Sunday afternoon, when the world is right. His rendering is freer than the illustrator-informed style of Winslow Homer and contains hints of the decorative, which must have appealed to the French artists Albert Marquet and Raoul Dufy, who saw and admired Prendergast's watercolors. Prendergast always suggests festivity, even though the figures are featureless and communication between individuals is usually very limited. Visual activity is elicited through the numerous small gestures which enliven the composition and display his inventive manner of handling his views of the world.

Whitney Museum of American Art, *Selections from the Lawrence H. Bloedel Bequest*, 1977, p. 43; Whitney Museum of American Art, New York, *Turn-of-the-Century America: Paintings, Graphics, Photographs 1890–1910*, 1977, p. 53; Whitney Museum of American Art, *Introduction to 20th Century Art: Selections from the Permanent Collection*, 1978, n.p.; Whitney Museum of American Art, *Maurice B. Prendergast: A Concentration of Works from the Permanent Collection of the Whitney Museum of American Art*, 1980, p. 32; Whitney Museum of American Art at Philip Morris, New York, *Urban Pleasures: New York 1900–1940*, 1986, n.p.

Edward Hopper

1882–1967

Dome, 1906–07 or 1909

Conté, wash, charcoal, and graphite on paper, 21⅜ x 19⅞ (54.3 x 50.5)

Josephine N. Hopper Bequest   70.1434

PROVENANCE

The artist

EXHIBITIONS

Presidential Life Insurance Company, Nyack, New York, *Edward Hopper/Nyack,* 1972; The Edward Hopper Landmark Preservation Foundation, Nyack, New York, *Welcome Home Edward Hopper,* 1976; Whitney Museum of American Art, New York, *Edward Hopper: The Art and the Artist,* 1980, p. 87 (traveled); Whitney Museum of American Art, New York, organizer, *The World of Edward Hopper: Selections from the Whitney Museum of American Art,* 1982, no. 71 (traveled in Australia); Whitney Museum of American Art, *Edward Hopper: Development of an American Artist,* 1983, n.p. (traveled)

Hopper's youthful trips to Paris greatly affected his art, though only briefly. He lost some of the dinginess his palette had acquired through the influence of Robert Henri, whose own style demonstrated an insipid version of Van Dyck and Velázquez. A friend, Patrick Henry Bruce, introduced Hopper to the work of the Impressionists and he soon developed a light airy palette which he employed for many years. His drawings, whether made in the countryside or in the Paris cafés, were mostly in charcoal, conté crayon, or pencil. The subject matter differed little from the usual tourist or illustrator's vignettes of the colorful life which animates the city streets.

Dome is a view of the Panthéon, seen from the Île de la Cité. Unlike his brightly colored paintings, Hopper's concurrent drawings indicate a penchant for deep secret shadows and bold compositions. The atmosphere, distinctly non-French, is of the kind that would emerge in his paintings of trees, isolated gas stations, and rows of buildings. Hopper catches the cold, milky gray climate of this wintery, damp northern city, as uninviting as the moiled Seine.

Hopper reduces the architecture to flat planes defined only by a selected use of highlights. Architecture was a theme he always responded to, quite possibly because of its impersonality and geometry. The pictorial device of running a barrier, in this instance the bridge, across the lower portion of the composition restrains the viewer from intimate access to the subject. This design device he continued to use with considerable frequency.

There is a secure, slow, pragmatic application of line in most of Hopper's drawings. The medium was for him always a practical exercise—it lead to prints or paintings. He often silhouettes, possibly as a result of his commercial art activities. The large bulking form in this drawing, stated in dense charcoal layerings, suggests a sense of abstraction. The conception of a city or townscape as a forbidding presence without any human reference is one that continues through his entire career. The best of his works seem to echo the old fairy tale line, "In the dark forest, dwelt. . . ."

Joseph Stella

1877–1946

An eclectic draftsman who in his long career employed several styles, probably concurrently, Joseph Stella was a prolific worker in all media, producing an enormous body of work including a series of brilliant silver-points. Initially self-taught, he came to New York from Italy in 1896, sponsored by his brother, a successful doctor. In New York, he studied at the Art Students League and at the New York School of Art. He also made many studies after Rembrandt in The Metropolitan Museum of Art.

While *Boy with Bagpipe* is dated 1910–12, it was possibly drawn earlier, because by 1911 Stella had traveled to Paris, where he encountered the modern art movement. This drawing is closer in style to those prevalent in late nineteenth-century Italy, with ideas of tonal control he could have learned in William Merritt Chase's classes at the New York School. Stella would always remain a brilliant manipulator of tonal contrasts, modeling his subjects either in black and white or in color. Even in his so-called Futurist-influenced works, such as those pertaining to the Brooklyn Bridge and other metropolitan images, he would rely on this aspect of his graphic skill to unify compositions.

The dramatic use of the broad textures describing the bagpipe and the suggestion of costume are in contrast to the carefully modulated tones that articulate the subject's face. The musician's outward glance brings the viewer inside the hazy atmospheric ambiance of the picture. It establishes an intimacy with the subject which animates the image. There is great firmness of hand, felt in even the sketchy aspects of composition. Some of the surface has been abraded by sandpaper to reduce the singularity of individually drawn lines by blending them into planar tones.

Boy with Bagpipe, 1910–12

Charcoal, pastel, and graphite on paper, 21 x 16 (53.3 x 40)

50th Anniversary Gift of Lucille and Walter Fillin   86.59

EXHIBITIONS

Whitney Museum of American Art, New York, *50th Anniversary Gifts*, 1980; WMAA 1981, p. 59; WMAA 1981a, n.p.; WMAA 1986, n.p.

Arthur G. Dove

1880–1946

Abstraction, Number 2, c. 1911

Charcoal on paper, 20⅝ x 17½
(52.4 x 44.5)

Purchase   61.50

PROVENANCE

The artist; The Downtown Gallery,
New York

EXHIBITIONS

School of Visual Arts, New York, 1963;
Heckscher Museum, Huntington, New
York, *Artists of Suffolk County Part II: The
Abstract Tradition*, 1970, p. 7; The Solomon
R. Guggenheim Museum, New York,
*Twentieth-Century American Drawing:
Three Avant-Garde Generations*, 1976,
p. 37; Whitney Museum of American Art,
New York, *Tradition and Modernism in
American Art: 1900–1930*, 1979; Terry
Dintenfass, Barbara Mathes, and Salander-
O'Reilly Galleries, New York, *Arthur
Dove: Paintings, Watercolors, Drawings,
Collages*, 1984

Among the few Americans who have successfully symbolized nature are
Charles Burchfield, Georgia O'Keeffe, and Arthur Dove. Their refined
hermetic methods of abstraction offered no stylistic inhibitions in the transcription of natural images; each one felt free to find individual patterns
and palettes.

In February 1912, the art dealer Alfred Stieglitz gave Dove his first one-
man exhibition. The works were presented as the first abstract, non-real-
istic art produced by an American. By this time, Dove had already given
such titles as *Nature Symbolized* or *Abstraction* to his paintings. He also
employed the term "lines of force," invented by Umberto Boccioni and in
use in European vanguard circles by 1911. Such lines might be observed
in *Abstraction, Number 2* of about 1911, a large charcoal sheet with many
of the shapes Dove would continue to use, even into the 1940s. Among
these are the so-called lines of force, and the saw-tooth-edged semicircle
across the lower part of the picture. The circles and the large configurations behind the force lines relate to the bulbous shapes which would
appear in a series of brightly colored pastels made in the following years.

By building his design on a rising arc, adding the extending radiating lines
which suggest rising as well as falling, Dove suggests the interplay between
the sky and the earth. If the circular shapes are abstracted trees or, as in
a later pastel, horses, they reaffirm the conviction that nature itself contains the major energy source for making art. Dove developed a method of
drawing a scene before him with a running line which engaged several
objects simultaneously. This produced the effect of a rather loosely formed
pattern. The application of nonnaturalistic color to the resulting design
often camouflaged the motif. The process produces an abstract picture,
though one still reminiscent of its sources. In developing this process, Dove
evolved a series of symbolic shapes which represent various aspects of his
psychological response to nature. This is similar in spirit to the shapes
devised by Burchfield, but Dove's are more on the order of hieroglyphs
and were probably made with less forethought than those of Burchfield.
Dove presents his experience of nature to augment our own experience
of her multitudinous aspects.

Georgia O'Keeffe

1887–1986

Modern art made an early impression on O'Keeffe. While a gifted student of William Merritt Chase at the Art Students League, she visited the Alfred Stieglitz gallery to see an exhibition of Rodin watercolors. Chase attacked the loosely made drawings of the French sculptor as weak, whereas O'Keeffe responded to them as displaying an open, free way of drawing. After leaving the League, she taught in various parts of the country, painting on her own. In 1914, at age twenty-seven, she reviewed her accomplishments and decided they lacked individuality. After destroying most of her work to that date, she made a decision to follow exactly the dictates of her imagination. From childhood she had used floral forms and it was to this world that she now turned for subject matter. She also decided to work in black and white until she had achieved a style to which color would come naturally. Her decisions also included the close and careful study of objects at a very short distance. An object from several feet away allows us to see it as a whole, while proximity reduces its individuality and produces a sense of intimacy and abstraction.

This magnified observation of nature produced many basic geometric shapes, including circles, spirals, and broad horizontals, rendered in a painterly manner. The spiral as the central form was to become a recurring motif that O'Keeffe found in plants, trees, and the curling smoke from trains seen across the desert and elsewhere. *Drawing No. 8* is the most fully rendered drawn image of her early modern years. It suggests the unfurling bracken shoots she might have seen in her wanderings in the Southwest. These abstractions, though derived from realistic sources, place her, along with Arthur Dove, in the forefront of the new art of this century.

These dramatic swirls—compacted, dense, bursting with nascent energy—constitute one of the most accomplished modern drawings made in America in the early years of the century. Yet for all its modernity, the drawing still employs the black border as a framing device, a technique used mostly by illustrators in the last decades of the nineteenth century. O'Keeffe soon eliminated this, placing her images on open sheets of paper, thus allowing an ever greater ambiguity in their reading and interpretation.

Drawing No. 8, 1915

Charcoal on paper mounted on cardboard, 24¼ x 18⅞ (61.6 x 47.9)

Purchase, with funds from the Mr. and Mrs. Arthur G. Altschul Purchase Fund 85.52

PROVENANCE

The artist; Robert Miller Gallery, New York

Thomas Hart Benton

1889–1975

What seemed to be Benton's natural craving for public response competed with his desire to make a place for himself in history. As a teenager, his cartoons won him fans in high school. After a brief art school interlude in Chicago, in 1908 he traveled to Paris and stayed for three years. There he met Stanton Macdonald-Wright as well as several noted French artists, and became interested in abstraction. Nevertheless, he was soon making sketches in the Louvre, studying compositions and the massing of light and dark in Old Master paintings. These were not slavish copies, but rough pencil drawings which would influence his teaching methods years later and which, at the time, constituted his method of finding inventive pictorial compositions.

"I had no interest in Parisian cubism. I didn't get interested in cubism until 1919, when it was a dead issue." Benton's so-called Cubist drawings were "all done after 1919 and they're based on the drawings of Cambiaso." *House in Cubist Landscape* is possibly one of the images made after his study of the sixteenth-century Genoese artist Luca Cambiaso, whose drawings often translate volumes into geometric solids. Although Benton had exhibited with the Synchromists in their 1916 New York exhibition, he showed paintings whose compositions were essentially derived from Michelangelo, though presented in a colorful modern palette. The exhibition, he later revealed, was a means of gaining attention in New York.

House in Cubist Landscape reflects Benton's natural sense for the manipulation of bulky shapes in space. His use of large simplified shapes, brightly colored and highly abstracted, is rare at this moment in American art. But he renounced abstraction after the winter of 1919–20. One wonders what might have happened had he not returned to a figural style incorporating genre subject matter in order to gain public recognition. Still, Benton always retained the skill of arranging large shapes in space, moving them in complicated compositional rhythms akin to those in the works of El Greco and the Baroque painters.

House in Cubist Landscape
(Landscape), c. 1919–20

Watercolor on paper mounted on board,
11¾ x 7¾ (29.8 x 19.7)

Purchase, with funds from The Hearst
Corporation   82.34

PROVENANCE

The artist; Charles Pollock; Salander-
O'Reilly Galleries, New York

EXHIBITIONS

WMAA 1985, p. 17

Charles Burchfield

1893–1967

Noontide in Late May, 1917

Watercolor and gouache on paper,
21⅝ x 17½ (54.9 x 44.5)

Purchase   31.408

PROVENANCE

The artist; Frank K. M. Rehn Gallery,
New York

EXHIBITIONS

Whitney Museum of American Art, New
York, *Charles Burchfield*, 1956, p. 16 (traveled); Bowdoin College Museum of Fine
Arts, Brunswick, Maine, 1958; Stamford
Museum and Nature Center, Connecticut,
Charles Burchfield Paintings, 1958; Santa
Barbara Museum of Art, California, *Painted
Papers: Watercolors from Dürer to the
Present*, 1962, n.p.; The Corcoran Gallery
of Art, Washington, D.C., *The New Tradition: Modern Americans Before 1940*, 1963,
p. 56; Whitney Museum of American Art,
*Pioneers of Modern Art in America: The
Decade of the Armory Show, 1910–1920*,
1963; High Museum of Art, Atlanta, *An
Anthology of Modern American Painting*,
1964, n.p.; Museum of Art, Munson-
Williams-Proctor Institute, Utica, New
York, *The Nature of Charles Burchfield: A
Memorial Exhibition*, 1970, n.p.; Andrew
Crispo Gallery, New York, *Ten Americans*,
1974, no. 17; Whitney Museum of American Art, *The Whitney Museum Studio Club
and American Art 1900–1932*, 1975, no. 23;
Whitney Museum of American Art, *Charles
Burchfield: A Concentration of Works
from the Permanent Collection of the Whitney Museum of American Art*, 1980, pp.
12–13; Whitney Museum of American Art,
Fairfield County, Stamford, Connecticut,
Pioneering the Century: 1900–1940,
1981, n.p.

Charles Burchfield was an artist who lived most of his life in small towns, yet he rarely painted the life of the town or its people, for nature was, in all her manifestations, Burchfield's great obsession. Sunlight, rain, fire-swept landscapes, moonlight, winter snow, the heat and the cold, are the themes that persist throughout his oeuvre. Rather than record the ordinary scene before him, Burchfield strove to use what he saw to communicate a wide range of human thought and feeling. *Noontide in Late May*, made by the artist in his mid-twenties, already suggests a mystical attitude toward nature. His simple method was to draw carefully with a pencil and enrich the image by the addition of watercolor or gouache. Oil painting never seemed to have been felicitious to his touch.

On the reverse of this drawing, Burchfield wrote: "An attempt to interpret a child's impression of noon-tide in late May—The heat of the sun streaming down, and rosebushes making the air drowsy with their perfume." In accomplishing his goal, he revealed the patterns he saw in nature. These were often laden with curious anthropomorphic suggestions. For Burchfield, nature remained a mystery to observe, experience, and explain.

Figurative artists usually contrive to isolate some significant object in an airy space, but Burchfield usually endows his compositions with the airless, heated atmosphere of deep summer or, in winter scenes, with a pervading airless chill. Seemingly arbitrary shapes are formed from what he sees in shadows, or from the sweeping gestures of the tree limbs touched by the wind. It could be argued that these patterning effects resulted from Burchfield's long employment as a wallpaper designer. But in fact he responds to a sense of growth, of urgent fecundity, of the need to follow nature's ancient rhythms. By nurturing his own spirit, Burchfield became one of our most significant artists.

Edward Hopper

1882–1967

Study for **Evening Wind,** 1921
Conté and charcoal on paper, 10 x 13^{15}⁄$_{16}$
(25.4 x 35.4)
Josephine N. Hopper Bequest   70.343

PROVENANCE

The artist

EXHIBITIONS

Presidential Life Insurance Company,
Nyack, New York, *Edward Hopper/
Nyack*, 1972; Hathorn Gallery, Skidmore
College, Saratoga Springs, New York, *The
Americans Circa 1952*, 1972, no. 10,
pp. 6–7; Whitney Museum of American
Art, New York, *Edward Hopper: Prints
and Illustrations*, 1979, pl. 78; Whitney
Museum of American Art, organizer,
Edward Hopper: The Formative Years,
1981 (traveled in Europe, catalogues in
Italian and German); Whitney Museum of
American Art, organizer, *The World of
Edward Hopper: Selections from the Col-
lection of the Whitney Museum of American Art*, 1982 (traveled in Australia), no.
75; Whitney Museum of American Art,
organizer, *Edward Hopper: Development
of an American Artist*, 1982, n.p. (traveled)

Between 1915 and 1928, Hopper produced a series of etchings and dry-
points, based on complex compositions first realized in drawings such as
Study for *Evening Wind*. As was his usual practice, he made the scale of
the drawing somewhat larger than that of the print he finally made from it.
The orientation of the drawing, however, is identical to that of the print.
Although his early prints are reverse images of the drawings, by about
1918 he was capable of turning the image in the mind's eye, as it would be
turned in the printing process. Most of the prints carefully follow the
drawing with only slight editing of the image. With the charcoal medium,
Hopper's lines yield a great tonal variety and texture, qualities lost in the
final print, whose sharper lines created a harsher light and more brittle
forms.

In Study for *Evening Wind,* a woman in a darkened room is climbing onto
a bed, before an open window whose billowing curtain signals the presence of the wind. She turns her head as if some sound or sight had caught
her attention in mid-action. There is no outside scene. Hopper's ability to
build solid compositional structures is apparent in the way in which the
external architectural element, seen through the window, forms a dramatic vertical element in the design. The curtain and the interior are held
in place by this device, whose rigidity contrasts with the softness of the
cascading curtain, the bedclothes, and the figure. Hopper's figure drawings, especially of the female, always suffer from excessive restraint, as if
he were held in thrall by the woman's emotional and intellectual complexities. He is more at ease with the architecture and the voluminous
curtain, which echoes the sails that so fascinated him. In these inanimate
things there is the sensuality one would normally expect to find in
drawings of the figure.

Louis Lozowick

1892–1973

Before leaving for a lengthy sojourn in Europe, Lozowick traveled to several American cities to get the flavor of the country, which he anticipated would become the subject of a series of paintings. In 1920 he traveled to Paris, the following year to Russia, later to Berlin, and then returned to the United States in 1924. Initially, this image of New York appeared as an oil sketch in 1922, followed by another in 1922–23, then as this drawing, as a lithograph of 1925 whose tones reverse those of the drawing, and as another painting in 1926–27. This 1923 drawing could well have been made in Berlin, where Lozowick had become acquainted with the Russian Constructivists and was especially friendly with El Lissitsky.

Lozowick combined the thrusting perspectives of his visionary drawings of New York, the Brooklyn Bridge, an elevated train station, and the metropolis' rising towers of office and residential buildings. His vision blends the geometric simplification of the American Precisionists with the dramatic graphic inventions of abstraction learned from the Constructivists. Through evenly balanced areas, bold design, and impersonal, mechanically produced line, Lozowick brought a rare modernity to images of the American scene. The careful tonal construction of each plane and its "color" in black, gray, or in the paper's tone, introduces a dense yet deep spatial experience that was extremely novel in the art of the time. This is not a documentary drawing, but a rendering of the artist's sensations of the city.

New York, c. 1923

Carbon pencil on paper, 12½ x 10
(31.8 x 25.4)

Purchase, with funds from the Richard and Dorothy Rodgers Fund   77.15

PROVENANCE

The artist; Artists Unlimited Gallery, New York

EXHIBITIONS

Whitney Museum of American Art, Downtown Branch, New York, *City Life 1910–1977: Selections from the Permanent Collection,* 1977, n.p.; Whitney Museum of American Art, Downtown Branch, *New York on Paper,* 1977, n.p.; WMAA 1978, p. 41; WMAA 1979, n.p.; Tokyo Metropolitan Art Museum, *Visions of New York City,* 1981, p. 64; Whitney Museum of American Art, Downtown Branch, *Lower Manhattan from Street to Sky,* 1982, n.p.

Elie Nadelman

1882–1946

Much of Nadelman's best sculpture is in carved wood. Yet he worked in many materials, among them plaster. This drawing seems to be after a destroyed, painted plaster, *Standing Woman in Hat* (c. 1921). The arc and curve were important drawing elements to Nadelman, for it was through them that he was able to achieve what he defined as harmony. A classical sense of unity is revealed in this programmatic use of these graphic marks.

The handling of pencil tone in *Head of a Woman with Hat* suggests the polychrome finish of the lost sculpture. A stylized head with a modern hairstyle, beneath a sweeping circular hat, argues for the identity of the woman as a noted social figure—Nadelman was famous for his portraits. However, though this drawing suggests a person, it is also carefully refined to render his idealized type. He rarely worked from a model, save when executing commissions. The sheet has the curious quality of looking as if it were drawn from life, yet at the same time suggesting the carved wood quality of Nadelman's sculpture.

The evenly drawn parallel hatching in varying densities of graphite defines planes and demarcates contrasting textures and materials. There is considerable variety in the function of Nadelman's lines, which enhances the vitality of the surface and image. These cautiously drawn lines move about the planes, defining areas to reveal a slow working method in keeping with the head's neoclassical austerity.

Head of a Woman with Hat, c. 1923–25

Graphite on vellum, 16½ x 10¾
(41.9 x 27.3)

Purchase, with funds from The Lily Auchincloss Foundation, Vivian Horan, The List Purchase Fund, the Neysa McMein Purchase Award, Mr. and Mrs. William A. Marsteller, the Richard and Dorothy Rodgers Fund, and the Drawing Committee
83.34

PROVENANCE

Estate of the artist; Zabriskie Gallery, New York; Barbara Mathes Gallery, New York

EXHIBITIONS

WMAA 1985, p. 40; WMAA 1986, n.p.

Theodore J. Roszak - 1925

Theodore Roszak

1907–1981

The artist's approach to drawing—its natural concerns, its methods and functions—may have changed more in the past eight decades of American art than at any time in history. This is dramatically revealed in the three drawings by Theodore Roszak in this exhibition.

In 1925 Roszak was a student at the School of the Art Institute of Chicago. He soon absorbed the tonal tradition taught there, which was derived from the fashionable styles of nineteenth-century Italy. Charcoal lines were blended into a smooth surface by using a stump, a tightly rolled pencil-shaped paper utensil which functions something like an eraser, to provide a nearly unbroken tonal surface. In depicting his music teacher, Roszak captures the personality of a man devoted to his sound structures and slightly removed from the everyday world. As in the academic tonal drawings students make from plaster-cast models, Roszak varies tonal densities and surface textures and modulates the use of light to reveal the personality of his sitter. While the camera's cycloptic vision lessens our knowledge of a subject through the evenness of its printed tones, colors, textures, and mechanical restrictions, drawing reveals not only the spirit and mind of the artist but also something of the subject.

A multitalented youth, Roszak struggled to choose between the demands of the muse of music and that of the fine arts. Music remained a significant factor in his life. The struggle is dramatically revealed in *Metaphysical Structure*, a modern fantasy constructed of biomorphic shapes and elements from musical instruments, with suggestions elicited from the human torso. Academic drawing at its best teaches rigorous skills which, in Roszak's case, allowed the clear presentation of ideas and feelings in very modern styles.

My Violin Teacher, 1925

Charcoal on paper, 21¼ x 16½ (54 x 41.9)

Gift of the Theodore Roszak Estate

83.33.4

PROVENANCE

Theodore Roszak Estate

EXHIBITIONS

WMAA 1985, p. 48; WMAA 1986, n.p.

Edward Hopper

1882–1967

Light at Two Lights, c. 1927

Watercolor on paper, 13¹⁵⁄₁₆ x 20
(35.4 x 50.8)

Josephine N. Hopper Bequest   70.1094

Hopper was an artist of periodic interests—his involvement with prints lasted only a few years, as did that with watercolor. He took up watercolor in 1923 for the first time since his student days, continuing with it for something over a decade before this medium also lost its appeal. By the late 1920s, Hopper had achieved his mature style, which is evident in his paintings as well as in the most finished of the watercolors. The house and the lighthouse of *Light at Two Lights* stand in isolation on a hill devoid of people or even the suggestion of human presence. There is a curious similarity between the shape of the top of the lighthouse and the dome which appears in the earlier Paris drawing.

Hopper's immediate appeal as always been his ability to formulate powerful dramatic compositions, as in *Light at Two Lights*. Isolated elements, seemingly unrelated to each other, fit together in an outdoor scene which, with a more romantic response to the subject, could easily have dissolved into a tourist-trade memento. Instead, Hopper suggests through the empty sky and these firmly developed images something of the isolation surely felt by the inhabitants of these buildings. He is a painter of moods, mostly dark ones. The massive, broad tone which stretches across the lower part of the composition blocks the viewer's easy access to the image. Hopper plies the page with such dark tones, forcing the light to emerge directly, boldly. The power of his images resides not in his refined skills, but in his transmission of felt experience.

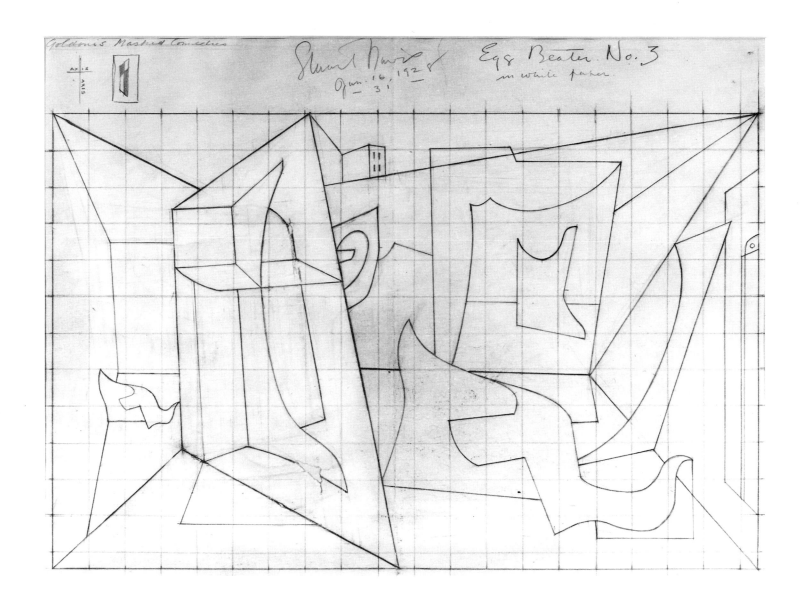

Goldoni's Masked Comedies

Stuart Davis
Jan. 16, 192?
— 31 —

Egg Beater No. 3
in white paper.

AXIS
AXIS

Stuart Davis

1894–1964

Through his father's association with Philadelphia newspapers, Davis came into contact with the newspapers' illustrators, some of whom went on to New York to join Robert Henri in the group known as The Eight. Davis' early drawings of street scenes or dance halls reflect the social subject matter that interested these artists. But in 1913, the Armory Show, in which he participated, suggested to him that the Henri approach to art was the end of a lingering tradition. Davis soon aimed at making pictures which were self-referential, even though they might examine views of the world. The subject was not the scene depicted, but the artist's interaction with that scene as it was transliterated through the abstract nature of the demands of the painting. In notes for a 1941 lecture, he wrote of the Egg-beater series, "In my 'eggbeater' pictures, which had a still life as subject matter, I equated all the forms and spaces of the subject in terms of flat, geometric shapes. I drew these planes in perspective and the result was what I would call a 'space-object.' " He continued: "The individual objects in the still life were visualized, not in their isolated internal aspects, but as part of a larger system of spatial relations and unity. These pictures derived from an emotional and imaginative perception of an objective matter; they included transposition of sizes, shapes, and colors, and were carried out in awareness of the logic of the three-dimensional color-space of the canvas."

Davis drew freehand. As the forms achieved the results he desired, he would sharpen the line and differentiate plane from plane with a straight-edge. A drawing which was made by responding to feelings is thereby given the look of a mechanical drawing. Evidence of many changes—erasures and pentimenti—remains on the page's worried surface. The grid was added afterward, for transfer, which makes its function different from that in the work of Chuck Close, who relies on the grid as a picture-structuring device.

Annotations are usual on many of Davis' drawings. "Goldoni's Masked Comedies" at upper left may refer to the eighteenth-century Italian play-wright Carlo Goldoni, and to the familiar costumes of the Commedia dell'Arte, with their geometric interlocking triangles of diverse colors. These are suggested in the axial structure of Davis' black-and-white draw-ing. His sensibility moved beyond Cubism to the manipulation of a flat surface pattern resembling that of the Neo-plastic painters. In the *Egg Beater No. 3* painting, individual shapes were painted in single colors with no tonal gradations.

Study for Eggbeater No. 3, 1928

Graphite and colored pencil on paper, 17 x 21⅜ (43.1 x 54.3)

Purchase, with funds from the Charles Simon Purchase Fund   80.46

PROVENANCE

Estate of the artist; Grace Borgenicht Gallery, New York

EXHIBITIONS

WMAA 1981, p. 17; WMAA 1981a, n.p.; WMAA 1982, n.p.

Charles Demuth

1883–1935

Distinguished Air, 1930

Watercolor on paper, 14 x 12 (35.6 x 30.5) sight

Purchase, with funds from the Friends of the Whitney Museum of American Art and Charles Simon   68.16

PROVENANCE

Estate of the artist; The Downtown Gallery, New York

EXHIBITIONS

The Art Galleries, University of California, Santa Barbara, *Charles Demuth: The Mechanical Encrusted on the Living,* 1971, n.p.; Andrew Crispo Gallery, New York, *Ten Americans: Masters of Watercolor,* 1975, n.p.; Whitney Museum of American Art, New York, *Selections from the Lawrence H. Bloedel Bequest,* 1977, p. 19; Whitney Museum of American Art, *William Carlos Williams and the American Scene: 1920–1940,* 1978, p. 70 (traveled); WMAA 1979, n.p.

It might be difficult these days to imagine a time when artists had a literary turn of mind. Charles Demuth was one such artist, who drew illustrations for many of the books he read, though few were published in his lifetime. Among those works he illustrated were Zola's *Nana,* Henry James' *The Turn of the Screw,* Frank Wedekind's *Erdgeist* and *Pandora's Box,* and tales by Balzac, Walter Pater, and Edgar Allan Poe. Late in life, he produced the most masterful illustration of all, a sheet for Robert McAlmon's short story *Distinguished Air.*

Published in Paris in 1925, *Distinguished Air* was the last book hand-printed by Bill Bird at his famous Three Mountains Press. The tales, according to McAlmon, recreate the time he spent in post-World War I Berlin with Marsden Hartley and reveal the life of "variant types with complete objectivity." Demuth, who was an intimate part of this circle, either read the story in a manuscript copy which circulated among the author's friends for years before publication, or in the book itself. Either way, it provided the occasion for him to produce one of his most ribald and colorful works. Five individuals stand admiring Brancusi's *Princess X.* As nearly always, Demuth drew his composition in pencil, carefully working in the watercolor and blotting it here and there to produce highlights and to break the surface planes. Most of his other illustrational drawings are quickly made sketchy affairs with watercolor washes added to heighten the effect. But *Distinguished Air* is equal to the quality and finish of his still-life and flower pieces. One need know nothing of its literary origins to accept it as a significant work by this master of the watercolor. The psychological interplay between members of this quintet is advertised in their gestures, postures, glances, and physical contact. This work represents the humanistic side of an artist who was also noted for his meticulous abstracted architectural renderings in the Precisionist manner.

Philip Guston

1913-1980

Drawing for **Conspirators,** 1930

Graphite, ink, colored pencil, and crayon on paper, 22½ x 14½ (57.2 x 36.8) irregular

Purchase, with funds from The Hearst Corporation and the Norman and Rosita Winston Foundation, Inc.   82.20

PROVENANCE

Estate of the artist; David McKee Gallery, New York

EXHIBITIONS

WMAA 1985, p. 28; Emily Lowe Gallery, Hofstra University, Hempstead, New York, *Maelstrom: Contemporary Images of Violence*, 1986, p. 5

Born in Montreal in 1913, Philip Guston went to Los Angeles in 1919 with his mother and siblings. His father followed soon thereafter and struggled to maintain the family, but five years later committed suicide. The youngest son was given a course in cartooning to occupy himself while recovering from the shock. Guston soon receded into an imaginary world developed through his drawings. As a student at Manual Arts High School, his best friend was Jackson Pollock. Both were expelled in about 1928 for devising a satirical broadside attacking the English department. In 1930 Guston was awarded a year's scholarship to the Otis Art Institute. After three months he abandoned the school and began to work on his own. His interest in Michelangelo, Mantegna, Giotto, Masaccio, and Piero della Francesca began in these difficult years and continued throughout his life.

As a participant in the John Reed Club, Guston responded to the members' Marxist urgings to forget "art for art's sake." The early effects of the Depression added substance to the club's pressure for political participation. The 1930 drawing for the *Conspirators* demonstrates Guston's socio-political concerns in its presentation of hooded Ku Klux Klan members at a lynching. The Klan had considerable visibility in California, where reports of their activities filled the newspapers. Guston produced in this drawing images which would continue to influence his art for decades. The hooded figure persisted into the period of the abstract paintings of the 1950s and reemerged in the late 1960s.

The boldly depicted anecdotalism reflects both Guston's interest in cartooning and its relationship to politics. A carefully conceived composition, the drawing is especially effective when we realize that the artist was seventeen years old. The large figure in the foreground fingers a thick rope which falls over a stylized shape representing the state of California, while next to it is another form suggesting a smaller southern state. This is art with a message treating a serious malaise of the day.

The wall serves as a background which boldly cuts through the pictorial space, thrusting the subjects toward the viewer. Secreted beneath their sheets, the huddled group converses, ignoring the deadly handiwork just above them. The dramatic modeling, with its sharp tonal transitions into deep darks, suggests sources in Michelangelo. Guston's design of the group of figures—condensed, flat, yet with a sense of bulky weightiness—differs from similar compositions by his early Italian influences, such as Giotto or Masaccio, in that the earlier artists used more open spatial conventions. Having absorbed the Italian Renaissance fresco tradition, Guston was soon to discover the Mexican mural movement and through the late 1930s became a successful mural painter himself.

Earle Horter

1891–1940

Earle Horter, a successful advertising artist, was friendly with Charles Demuth, Charles Sheeler, and other Precisionist painters. The direction of his own art was often influenced by his associates. Among the most accomplished of his drawings is *The Chrysler Building Under Construction*, the idea for which might have been suggested by Sheeler's *Delmonico Building* (1927). Although Horter was too eclectic in his aesthetic moods to become an influential artist, this rigorous modern drawing, with its careful combination of straightedge drawing and watercolor in-painting to define a thrusting composition, is a brilliant example of the new Precisionist art. New York skyscrapers are perfect subject matter for the rigid geometry of Precisionism. Horter's use of light to define and direct our eye through the composition augments the rising perspectives of the Chrysler Building, as viewed from 42nd Street near Third Avenue. He captures the lively metropolitan spirit of one of the city's great buildings. This is a finely wrought watercolor by an artist whose body of work remains relatively unknown and unstudied.

The Chrysler Building Under Construction, 1931

Ink and watercolor on paper, 20¼ x 14¾ (51.4 x 37.5)

Purchase, with funds from Mrs. William A. Marsteller   78.17

PROVENANCE

Mrs. Earle Horter; Robert Schoelkopf Gallery, New York

EXHIBITIONS

WMAA 1978, p. 33; WMAA 1979, n.p.; Tokyo Metropolitan Art Museum, *Visions of New York City*, 1981, p. 54; Whitney Museum of American Art, New York, organizer, *American Art of the 1930s: Selections from the Collection of the Whitney Museum of American Art*, 1981, p. 26 (traveled); Whitney Museum of American Art at Philip Morris, New York, *On 42nd Street: Artists' Visions*, 1984, no. 1

Arshile Gorky

1905–1948

Arshile Gorky, a naturally gifted draftsman, drew throughout his career. Sporadically he would concentrate on drawing, the results of which would have a significant impact on the development of his art. In the early 1930s, he began a series of studies for a mural for which there seems to be no record of a potential commission. The large number of drawings in this series were made with pen and ink, always in black and white. The full mural study is a low, horizontal compartmentalized design, loosely based on the design of *The Profanation of the Host* by Paolo Uccello. Gorky produced many studies for individual sections of this mural. *Nighttime, Enigma and Nostalgia* is an examination of approximately two-thirds of the left side of the composition, enlarged, refined, and transformed.

It is from these early drawings that Gorky developed the rhythmic line which is so admired in his later works. In these pages, he demonstrated his facility for synthesizing the multiple sources to which he responded, such as the works of Uccello, Cézanne, Picasso, Miró, Ernst, and others. Yet Gorky always produced a work bearing his own stamp. The large drawings that examine sections of the mural represent some of the most innovative and complex early abstract drawings made in America. His thought restructured the relationships of some elements, changed the role of light, and shifted emphasis from area to area. Biomorphism, a transformation of imagery through the use of flowing lines that frequently produce a layering of transparencies, engenders abstract images. Whether this flowing line delineates the palette-shaped forms set in a dusky Surrealist ambiance on the left, or the shapes that suggest a couple locked in an embrace at the top center, or the striding figure on the right, it is played off against the rigorous black background hatchings or the hard-ruled lines on the right. Gorky's use of compartmentalization suggests interdependence rather than isolation. These multiple images display a searching awareness, almost as if his imagination were racing ahead of him, driving him to greater invention through the production of more drawings. That energy and the enrichment of his passionate invention still enhances our experience of his art.

Nighttime, Enigma and Nostalgia,
c. 1931–32
Ink on paper, 24 x 31 (61 x 78.7)

50th Anniversary Gift of Mr. and Mrs. Edwin A. Bergman   80.54

EXHIBITIONS

Whitney Museum of American Art, New York, *50th Anniversary Gifts*, 1980; The Solomon R. Guggenheim Museum, New York, *Arshile Gorky: A Retrospective*, 1981, no. 45; WMAA 1981, p. 23; WMAA 1982, n.p.

Charles Sheeler

1883–1965

Interior, Bucks County Barn, 1932

Crayon on paper, 15 x 18¾
(38.1 x 47.6) sight

Purchase   33.78

PROVENANCE

The artist

EXHIBITIONS

The Currier Gallery of Art, Manchester, New Hampshire, *Exhibition of Contemporary American Drawings*, 1956; Addison Gallery of American Art, Phillips Academy, Andover, Massachusetts, *The American Line: 100 Years of Drawing*, 1959, p. 88; The Morse Gallery of Art, Rollins College, Winter Park, Florida, *Exhibition of 20th-Century American Drawings*, 1962; Museum of Art, Pennsylvania State University, University Park, *Charles Sheeler: The Works on Paper*, 1974, p. 77; Kunsthaus Zurich, *Malerei und Photographie im Dialog*, 1977, p. 405; WMAA 1979, n.p.; Whitney Museum of American Art, New York, *Stuart Davis, Charles Sheeler, Joseph Stella*, 1979; Whitney Museum of American Art, *Charles Sheeler: A Concentration of Works from the Permanent Collection of the Whitney Museum of American Art*, 1980, p. 26; Whitney Museum of American Art, organizer, *American Art of the 1930s: Selections from the Collection of the Whitney Museum of American Art*, 1981, p. 28 (traveled); The Hudson River Museum, Yonkers, New York, *Form or Formula: Drawing and Drawings*, 1986, p. 49

For years Charles Sheeler made his livelihood as a professional photographer of portraits and objects in museum collections. He was also occasionally commissioned to record industrial sites and architecture. His concurrent painting is frequently described as Precisionism, a style which is pristine, wholesome, and pragmatic. Most of his art is carefully made and balanced, eliciting responses similar to those generated by the appreciation of still life.

The source of *Interior, Bucks County Barn* is a photograph Sheeler made around 1915, which is so closely followed in the drawing that one wonders whether he employed an opaque projector. Yet Sheeler's transformation of the photographic image is startling. The photograph reveals a broken-down carriage in a dirty dilapidated barn where the interior light is dusky and the light from outside coldly brilliant. Sheeler enhanced the drawing by expanding the role of light, which now illumines clean smooth surfaces and crisply defined planes and edges. He invented a broad series of textures to identify each of the many surfaces. The interior, instead of displaying the lugubrious grays of the photograph, has walls brilliant with light, which define the sharp, hard-edge demarcations of the buggy as well as of the framing door. The machinery on the left side of the composition, poorly defined in the photograph, is quickened by sharp textural differentiations and the specificity with which each element is drawn.

The artist's editing process—selecting which elements to remove from the photograph and which to emphasize—has produced a drawing which, while time-consuming in its technique, is an exciting interpretation of a nostalgic scene. The drawing intensifies the experience of a subject which in its photographic state would be overlooked. It remains one of Sheeler's most accomplished graphic works.

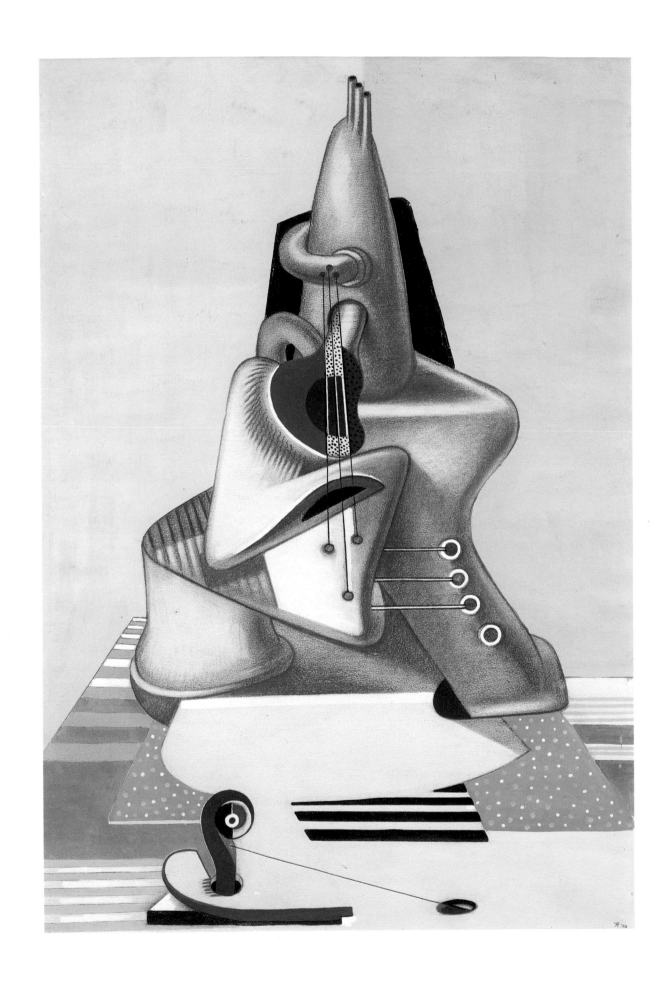

Theodore Roszak

1907–1981

Between 1929 and 1931, Roszak traveled in Europe on a scholarship from the School of the Art Institute of Chicago. He visited several countries, finally settling in Prague for nine months. There he came into contact with modern art and architecture, discovering the work of de Chirico, Klee, Picasso, Léger, the Constructivists, and the Surrealists. The experience made him an exponent of modernism. Thereafter, he infused increasing degrees of abstraction into his work and in 1936 turned to non-figural Constructivist abstractions. He continued painting, but publicly he was to be known as a sculptor.

A prolific draftsman, Roszak explored his compositions in fragmental studies, building and revising images into larger, fully rendered configurations. During the 1930s, he was still struggling with the choice between becoming a musician and a visual artist. This conflict is the source of the imagery of *Metaphysical Structure*. The drawing also reveals the modern influences Roszak garnered from his European experience. The free-formed monument is a Surreal combination of musical instruments and body parts that generate an aerodynamic biomorphic shape. The patterned landscape is a curious comment on late Cubist painting, which had devolved into decoration. Yet, while abstraction continued to imbue Roszak's work with formal structural concerns, he remained influenced by nature and man's interrelation with it.

Metaphysical Structure, 1933

Crayon, gouache, and ink on paper,
23 x 26⁹⁄₁₆ (58.4 x 67.5)

Gift of the Theodore Roszak Estate
83.33.5

PROVENANCE

Theodore Roszak Estate

EXHIBITIONS

WMAA 1985, p. 49

Jackson Pollock

1912–1956

In June 1930, Pollock saw the newly completed fresco, *Prometheus*, by José Clemente Orozco at Pomona College. In September, Pollock registered in the Thomas Hart Benton evening class at the Art Students League, where he remained for two years. For most of the Depression years, he worked on one of the various government programs established to aid artists. He also found time to spend a part of each summer with Benton on Martha's Vineyard.

The imagery in Pollock's art rises from multiple sources. Benton's teaching methods stressed composition, a linear rhythmic drawing system, and the formation of bulking shapes in the design. The glyphic vocabulary of Western American Indians and the Mexican mural painters, especially Orozco, also claimed Pollock's interest. During his study with Benton, moreover, he evolved a style which evoked the influence of Albert Pinkham Ryder.

In the late 1930s, Pollock suffered from severe alcoholism and underwent treatment by several Jungian psychiatrists. At least one of them instructed him to produce drawings to help reveal the content of his troubled unconscious. Most of these therapeutic works are similar in technique and content to the studio-made art.

Untitled is a powerful study in dark and light contrasts, formed by demarcations in long striated compound lines augmented by close dark hatching. It is difficult to ascertain whether this composition is an invention on Pollock's part or relates to paintings seen in The Metropolitan Museum of Art, where Benton often sent his students to draw. Pollock employed the abstract graphic approach recommended by his teacher, rather than developing an anecdotal subject matter.

Untitled, c. 1933–39

Graphite and colored crayon on paper,
15 x 10 (38.1 x 25.4)

Purchase, with funds from the Julia B. Engel Purchase Fund and the Drawing Committee 85.17

PROVENANCE

Lee Krasner Pollock Estate; Jason McCoy Inc., New York

EXHIBITIONS

WMAA 1985, p. 43

Marsden Hartley

1877–1943

In the late 1920s, Hartley produced a series of silverpoint drawings in emulation of Cézanne's carefully hatched depictions of Mont-Sainte-Victoire and other locations in the south of France. From the autumn of 1933 into the early winter of 1934, he returned to his meditations on the French artist in a series of drawings and paintings made in the Bavarian town of Garmisch-Partenkirchen. Hartley walked the country roads, exploring sites, drawing views that appealed to him, then returning to the studio to paint. In this drawing, the lessons of Cézanne have been assimilated and combined with other mark-making systems. Individual aspects of the mountains are depicted in a bold, broken outline, with areas of tonal hatching firmly laid within them. The textual striations suggest tree-covered slopes without attempting individual depiction. By varying the pressure on the charcoal stick, Hartley shifts from deep black to light grays, thereby introducing the "colors" of black and white. The spaces between the closely hatched lines vary the density of the surface, allowing for an atmospheric perspective, similar to that found in Oriental prints. The distant mountain tops are drawn in a blended tonal manner. This softness of tone and the open areas of the paper suggest a distant light, which is counterbalanced by the dark, dense forms in the lower half of the composition.

Hartley's use of line underwent an evolution during his long career. It would have been difficult at this moment to foresee that his later work would take on an increasingly expressionistic force and a crude finish quite unlike the intelligent refinement of these mid-career drawings.

Alspitze, c. 1934

Charcoal on paper, 13 x 9¹³⁄₁₆ (33 x 24.9)

Purchase, with funds from the Equitable Life Assurance Society of the United States Purchase Fund   84.33

PROVENANCE

The artist; Joshua Strychalski; Mr. and Mrs. Carl D. Lobell; Barbara Mathes Gallery, New York

EXHIBITIONS

Barbara Mathes Gallery, New York, *Early 20th-Century American Works on Paper*, 1984; WMAA 1985, p. 28

Grant Wood

1891–1942

Grant Wood is the most refined exemplar of the tradition which repudiated modernism in America until well into the 1940s. He was a member of the generation that feared modern art and, in defiance, harked back to an arts and crafts tradition as well as to that of the Old Masters. Craft was of primary importance and, following that, conservative imagery and techniques. With the rise of modernism and the loss of patronage by the church, the state, or powerful families, commissions were no longer a general source of support; the espousal of an individual style became the necessary hallmark of one's productivity.

In this context, Wood looked to Europe for traditions which would offer succor. He responded to the Northern artists with their refined drawing, clear forms, and crystalline light. His carefully delineated figures stand before the landscape, almost like cutouts and as if in anticipation of the minimal forms of abstract artists of nearly half a century later. Wood's drawing line and the surface texture are also surprisingly similar to that of Seurat and stand in startling contrast to the historical perspective which informs his subject matter.

Study for *Breaking the Prairie,* designed for a mural in Ames, Iowa, is one of his largest extant colored drawings. A long panel with two vertical wings, it depicts the breaking of the prairie sod after the felling of its forest cover. Oxen cut the first difficult furrows, followed by horses. Wood animates his composition by implied vertical arcs in each of the end panels, which return the eye to the central panel. This panel, with its teams moving in opposite directions, produces a feeling of cross-purposes, while the stylized clouds contain and stabilize the composition. The flowers in the lower portion of the design are especially effective in their drawing and color, revealing a close study from nature.

Study for **Breaking the Prairie,** c. 1935–39

Colored pencil, chalk, and graphite on paper, 22¾ x 80¼ (57.8 x 203.8)

Gift of Mr. and Mrs. George D. Stoddard
81.33.2a–c

PROVENANCE

Estate of the artist; Mr. and Mrs. George D. Stoddard

EXHIBITIONS

WMAA 1978, p. 63; Whitney Museum of American Art, New York, *William Carlos Williams and the American Scene: 1920–1940,* 1979, p. 126–27 (traveled); Whitney Museum of American Art, Fairfield County, Stamford, Connecticut, *Pioneering the Century: 1900–1940,* 1981, n.p.; The Minneapolis Institute of Arts, *Grant Wood: The Regionalist Vision,* 1983, p. 167 (traveled)

Charles Biederman

b. 1906

In his early twenties, Charles Biederman studied at the School of the Art Institute of Chicago, where, in the galleries, he was attracted to the modern pictures in the Birch Bartlett collection. His interest in abstraction may have begun with these paintings; it reached fruition during his first European travels. As early as December 1, 1935, the twenty-nine-year-old artist wrote in a letter: "I am working for a complete riddance of any semblance to nature objects in my painting." Between 1935 and 1936, Biederman lived in New York. He declined an invitation to join the American Abstract Artists because of its national, rather than international, ambitions. A growing interest in Léger, whose work he admired, led him to refine his drawing to an even greater extent. There was a brief period of exploration of biomorphic shapes that occasionally seemed to float in an indeterminate space. These were succeeded by imagery inspired by machine tools, such as that in *New York, February 1936*. This carefully constructed composition is mature, complicated, individual, and inventive. Through the use of color as a form-building or form-defining device, Biederman was able to achieve works that were far ahead of those being produced by non-objective artists in America. His plasticity of form differs from the relatively flat surfaces not only of American, but also of European abstractionists. Moreover, Biederman's work was more boldly dramatic in scale and his colors harsher and brighter than those of his European contemporaries.

Biederman visited the 1937 Paris World's Fair and found the technical exhibits more stimulating than the art exhibitions. This discovery formed his resolve to change from painter into "structuralist." It was in 1937 that he ceased to "draw, paint or sculpt," and began to "use the new medium of art—the machine." Biederman's growing engagement with a machine aesthetic—that is, one with the gestural traces of the human hand eliminated, implying non-textured surfaces, ruled edges, and closely grained shading—becomes apparent in the drawing process. In order to fulfill the potential of his discovery, he retired to a country life in southern Minnesota, essentially isolating himself from the world of art. During these years he produced some of the most innovative art to be seen in America. His writings elicited a considerable following in England and Europe, which soon encouraged public interest in his art in America. But it is only within the past decade that his structures have found a wider public. Biederman remains a classic example of isolated American genius, producing an art of subtle dynamics.

New York, February 1936, 1936

Gouache on composition board,
29¹⁵/₁₆ x 21³/₁₆ (76 x 53.8)

Purchase, with funds from the Drawing Committee   85.57

PROVENANCE

The artist; Grace Borgenicht Gallery, New York

Federico Castellon

1914–1971

In 1932, the Julien Levy Gallery presented the first American Surrealist exhibition in New York City. Thereafter, almost annually, exhibitions of Surrealist work were to be seen either in the galleries or at The Museum of Modern Art. In 1934, Dali made his first trip to the city, instilling his own ideas, images, and personality into the art scene. The exhibitions stimulated a considerable response among young artists, especially those looking for an aesthetic approach outside of geometric abstraction.

Federico Castellon, born in Spain in 1914, was brought to America when he was seven years old to reside with his family in Brooklyn. As a youth he drew, showing evidence of considerable talent. Essentially an autodidact in art, he attended only a few classes at the Art Students League. By his early twenties, he had achieved a mature style which responded to the seductive appeal of Surrealism, especially that of Dali. In the mid-1930s, a two-year stay in France brought him into even closer contact with the masters of this literary art. The subtle influence of the dream also has a long tradition in American art, from Thomas Cole to Charles Burchfield, and down to Jonathan Borofsky in our own day.

Surrealism juxtaposes contradictions to engender its nervous responses. Castellon's *The Bed* is a tonal pencil drawing of a pandiculated male figure reclining in bed, set in a desert landscape. He is accompanied by a nude female figure and a biomorphic chair draped in swags of rent cloth, from whose orifices protrude a crabbed hand and a tree branch with a box in its upper limbs. This box, of fragmented interior planes, reveals a secreted portrait. The hirsute male figure holds in one palsied hand a mass of hair that serves as a bed shawl. The bleeding bed drains into a wooden bowl which has a carefully drilled hole that allows its contents to exude onto the desert floor. In the central foreground stands a bizarre assortment of quasi-anthropomorphic shapes, seemingly made of clay, which could represent an isolated landscape within the larger configuration. Among the other strange images is the shoe, a noted fetishistic symbol, protruding from the man's rotted swaddlings.

Like Ionesco, Castellon peoples his stage with characters who rise from an obscure past, unaware of the portents of the future. The skillful drawing technique employs a variety of gray tones, much as we see in black and white photographs. But a milky light reveals the various objects in a clarity rarely obtainable in photography. Castellon provides his own complete vision of the world in a Surrealist-informed vocabulary that is very much his own achievement.

The Bed, 1937

Graphite on paper, 10¼ x 13 (26 x 33)

Gift of Mr. and Mrs. Benjamin Weiss
78.38

EXHIBITIONS

WMAA 1978, p. 23; WMAA 1979, n.p.; International Exhibitions Foundation, organizer, *Twentieth-Century American Drawings: The Figure in Context*, 1984, p. 38 (traveled)

Burgoyne Diller

1906–1965

Diller was not a prolific artist, and there was little understanding of his art because he undertook a form of expression which had few if any supporters; indeed, he sold not one picture during the 1930s. He was one of the first artists in America to respond to the art of the Russian Constructivists and to Neo-plastic painting. By 1930, when he left the Art Students League, he had begun his first geometric style work. In 1933, evidence of de Stijl influence became strikingly apparent in his paintings.

A year later, Diller began a series of wood constructions composed of painted slats of wood, layered over a painted surface with space between the layers. *Second Theme*, a drawing of 1938 which examines similar motifs, suggests a spatial arrangement related to that of the constructions. Diller achieves the effect of depth and space by introducing wide, dramatic linear forms, painted in different colors which cross over one another. With this spatial reading, he radically changed the system employed by the Neo-plastic and Constructivist painters.

Although he was acquainted with the theories of many European artists, as well as with Platonic and Eastern philosophies, Diller was not constrained to follow rules. Therefore proportion, an important structural element in his work, is not the result of an applied intellectual scheme directed toward pictorial resolution, but of a judicial placement conceived by an informed eye. The peripheral lines might well be drawn by a straightedge, but their width is elected by eye to create a sense of dynamic visual tension. After designing the composition of these panels, Diller applied color by using a simple repeated gesture. He is not an artist whose hand is clearly discernible in his drawings, and this very anonymity supports the intellectual aspects of his compositions.

Many of Diller's drawings are bordered by a wide area of dense graphite. Within this border, which acts to isolate the image from the page, is the drawing. *Second Theme*, because it appears cognate with Diller's constructions, suggests receding space behind the picture plane. The bold vertical on the left and the bar across the lower section of the design are easily balanced by the smaller linear bars, the color, and the spatial configurations. In *Second Theme*, one of Diller's largest complete presentation drawings, we experience an art filled with the innate American sense of open space.

Second Theme, 1938

Graphite and crayon on paper, 12½ x 12¾ (31.8 x 32.4)

Purchase, with funds from the List Purchase Fund   79.5

PROVENANCE

The artist; Meredith Long Contemporary, New York

EXHIBITIONS

WMAA 1979, n.p.; The Drawing Center, New York, *Sculptors' Drawings Over Six Centuries*, 1981; Whitney Museum of American Art, New York, organizer, *American Art of the 1930s: Selections from the Collection of the Whitney Museum of American Art*, 1981 (traveled); WMAA 1981, p. 19; Whitney Museum of American Art, Fairfield County, Stamford, Connecticut, *Pioneering the Century: 1900–1940*, 1981, n.p.

Stuart Davis

1894–1964

By the late 1930s, Davis had developed a brightly hued palette. He would often employ wide colored lines over seemingly arbitrary color shapes derived from a motif. In a statement that aligns him with Whistler, the Neo-plastic painters, and some of his contemporary abstractionists, he declared his interests to be color and space harmonies. Of the painting *Bass Rocks,* he wrote, "Casual observation of the scene from which they were taken would not reveal the elements from which my picture is made. These harmonies only become apparent after study and contemplation of it. I think this is its chief value, that it is a record of certain hidden beauties, which are none the less true and real." An artist's statement such as this can often provide a guide to his thinking, but can rarely explain a work of art. Nevertheless, Davis' work is now seen as one of the most modern expressions of the American Scene—the city, the countryside, seashore, and architecture, but rarely people.

A programmatic worker, Davis' usual practice was to sketch a scene, redraw it in a stylized manner, paint a small gouache drawing, sometimes draw an ink version, apply a grid for transfer, and then produce a painting. In the process, he flattened the space and introduced wandering lines or areas of color.

As a polemicist for modernism, Davis developed his own theories and urged others to do the same. He rarely veered into total abstraction. His vision of the world was a jazzy baroque one—flecks of hot color, shifting perspectives, and changing color-spatial relationships. This drawing is one of two studies for the painting *Bass Rocks.* The colors vary among the three works but the angular shapes remain the same, as do the linear descriptive lines. It can be assumed from the color changes that Davis was striving to increase the visual activity of the composition. Since color can be read as having different spatial densities or weights, he would change the color of a line as it crossed into another area of color. "A line," Davis remarked in 1940, "must always be thought of as a *place* where *something is going on.*"

Study for **Bass Rocks,** 1939

Gouache on board, 11⁹⁄₁₆ x 14 (29.4 x 35.6)

Gift of Jerome Zipkin   81.41

PROVENANCE

The artist; The Downtown Gallery, New York; Jerome Zipkin

EXHIBITIONS

WMAA 1985, p. 22

Edwin Dickinson

1891–1978

Edwin Dickinson's accomplishments synthesized the dramatically contrasting aesthetics of his two teachers—the bold compositional concepts of William Merritt Chase and the tonal romanticism of Charles Hawthorne. Dickinson is a rare American master of sfumato, the achievement of tonal atmospheric effects. He was, for a time, a sailor and lived most of his life by the sea. It therefore was natural for him to study the hazes, the fogs, the shaken light rebounding from the waves' edges, or the myriad broken reflections cast off by the sea's shining surface.

Still life is a continuing American tradition, often relying on readily found, homely objects. The hushed house in *Roses,* with its partially lowered shades, is full of the half-lights Dickinson favored. His drawing methods evidence little change through his career. Forms are set in tonal washes of charcoal, then defined by a sharp, hard pencil line, as fragile as it is meticulous in its definitions. Highlights are brushed into the composition either by the use of a stump, a rag, or the artist's finger.

Roses, a work of Dickinson's middle period, exhibits his best qualities. The smoky tones suggest the elegant Edwardian style rather than Victorian crankiness. The light appears to emerge less from the window, with its gray vista, than from the flowers themselves. Individual petals appear carved from the crumbly gray background. For all this delicacy, many of Dickinson's drawings nevertheless emanate a sensual solidity as striking as white marble in sunlight. Although he failed his mathematical examination for the U.S. Naval Academy in 1909, he retained a sense of mathematical structure as a working aspect of his compositional dynamics. It is the romantic, light-filled quality of his drawings that softens the subject matter, whereas his paintings display a formal and calculated finish.

Roses, 1939

Graphite on paper, 10¾ x 12¾
(27.3 x 32.4)

Promised 50th Anniversary Gift of
Mrs. Robert M. Benjamin   P.6.80

EXHIBITIONS

Whitney Museum of American Art, New
York, *50th Anniversary Gifts*, 1980;
WMAA 1981, p. 17

Reginald Marsh

1898–1954

New Dodgem, 1940

Watercolor on paper, 40½ x 26¾
(102.9 x 68) sight

Gift of the artist, and gift of Gertrude
Vanderbilt Whitney, by exchange   53.21

PROVENANCE

The artist

EXHIBITIONS

The Museum of the City of New York,
Exhibition of Coney Island Subjects, 1954;
Whitney Museum of American Art, New
York, *Reginald Marsh*, 1955, n.p. (traveled); Whitney Museum of American Art,
Reginald Marsh, 1956, n.p. (traveled);
Huntington Art Galleries, West Virginia, *50
Paintings from the Collection of the Whitney Museum of American Art*, 1958; Santa
Barbara Museum of Art, California, *Painted
Papers—Watercolors from Dürer to Our
Time*, 1962; University Art Gallery, University of Arizona, Tucson, *Reginald Marsh
Retrospective*, 1969; Whitney Museum of
American Art, *Seven Decades of 20th-
Century American Art*, 1969; Whitney
Museum of American Art, Downtown
Branch, New York, *City Life 1910–1977:
Selections from the Permanent Collection*,
1977, n.p.; WMAA 1979, n.p.; Whitney
Museum of American Art, Downtown
Branch, *New York on Paper*, 1977, n.p.;
Whitney Museum of American Art, *Decade
of Transition: 1940–1950*, 1981, n.p.;
Whitney Museum of American Art at Philip
Morris, New York, *Reginald Marsh's New
York*, 1983, p. 98 (traveled); Museum of
the Borough of Brooklyn at Brooklyn College, New York, *Fun and Fantasy: Brooklyn's Amusement Parks and Leisure Areas*,
1984

A member of a generation that still venerated the Old Masters while rejecting new art, Reginald Marsh reveled in providing entertaining subject matter. His upper middle-class background notwithstanding, he searched out the seedy if not the seamy side of life, whether it was the display of animated oiled bodies on Coney Island beaches, or the midway shows with their thrill rides and strip-tease theatricals, or the teeming life along Fourteenth Street and the Bowery. The sketchbook was Marsh's diary. Like a good reporter getting the facts, he would fill pages with images to be expanded into larger compositions in the studio. *New Dodgem*, a large composition of his mature years, demonstrates his interest and concerns in the fullness of his style. The writhing mass of figures in the foreground appears in stark contrast to the heavy rigid architecture above.

Marsh preferred liquid media. The pen or brush always moved with ease over the page, responding to his natural inclination toward curves and a plenitude of form. His style is built on a simple underdrawing, over which he applies dark and light washes in an elegant, active play of light and shadow. He stated in a 1934 letter to his friend and patron William Benton that in his art "Muscles is [sic] the key note." He was an obsessive draftsman of the figure, in time evolving a line which was tapered and swelling, like that employed by reproductive engravers. Marsh remains a genre painter always concerned with charming his audience. His version of Social Realism lacks political importunings, and is closer to that of the pin-up than even to the simple anecdotalism of his contemporaries, the Regionalists. It is an art of a simple bygone world now relished with nostalgia.

Willem de Kooning

b. 1904

The combination of de Kooning's innate talent and his rigorous training at the Rotterdam Academy of Fine Arts developed his sure hand at drawing. He also has a great gift for formal pictorial invention. *Manikins*, a pencil drawing of two standing men, may be based on store-window dummies or it could as easily represent figures at a subway stop flanking a support column. The drawing demonstrates de Kooning's neoclassic drawing skills in the fine rendering of the figure on the right, which stands in contrast to the expressionist finish given to the figure on the left. Although this latter figure manifests the same controlled hand, the facial treatment and contour tones of the upper torso are stated in gritty linear textures.

This bifurcated stylistic approach pervades de Kooning's work. In this drawing, which can also be read as two versions of a self-portrait, we note a biomorphic influence in the handling of the men's suits. These shapes would be developed in the black-and-white paintings of the late 1940s. The accentuated eyes, dilated nostrils, and other facial features prefigure the approach to physiognomy that emerged in the painting *Woman* (1948) and was fully explored in the Women series of the 1950s. A natural ability to instill characterization is detected even in the sketchy figure on the far left, which may be a poster, a figure in a miror, or, if the figures are store-window dummies, a passer-by looking in.

In his search for an individual vocabulary, de Kooning eschewed systems and standard methodologies. *Manikins* contains the seeds of many future figural and abstract aspects of his art. Because he destroyed many of his early drawings, it is impossible to construct an accurate reading of his development. *Manikins* remains an early example of his striving for individuality.

Manikins, c. 1942

Graphite on paper, 13½ x 16¼
(34.3 x 41.3)

Purchase, with funds from the Grace Belt Endowed Purchase Fund, the Burroughs Wellcome Purchase Fund, the H. van Ameringen Foundation, The Norman and Rosita Winston Foundation, Inc., and the Drawing Committee 84.5

PROVENANCE

The artist; Xavier Fourcade Gallery, New York

EXHIBITIONS

Whitney Museum of American Art, New York, *Willem de Kooning: Drawings, Paintings, Sculpture,* 1984, p. 35 (traveled); WMAA 1985, p. 23

Morris Graves

b. 1910

Journey, 1943

Gouache and watercolor on paper,
22¼ x 30⅛ (56.5 x 76.5) sight

Purchase   45.14

PROVENANCE

The artist; Willard Gallery, New York

EXHIBITIONS

Walker Art Center, Minneapolis, *Reality
and Fantasy: 1900–1954,* 1954, p. 9; American Federation of Arts, New York, *The
Drawings of Morris Graves,* 1960, no. 2
(traveled); University of Oregon Museum
of Art, Eugene, *Morris Graves: A Retrospective,* 1966, p. 54; Witte Memorial Museum, San Antonio, Texas, *Morris Graves,*
1969, n.p.; The National Museum of Art,
Osaka, Japan, *Pacific Northwest Artists
and Japan,* 1982, p. 43; Whitney Museum
of American Art, New York, *Decade of
Transition: 1940–1950,* 1981, n.p.; The
Phillips Collection, Washington, D.C.,
*Morris Graves: The Vision of the Inner
Eye,* 1983, no. 58 (traveled)

Many American artists avoid living in large cities, especially the art centers, choosing instead to reside in small towns or in rural areas. One of
these is Morris Graves, who has spent most of his life in the country in the
vicinity of Seattle or traveling in the green glades of Ireland or England
and recently in northern California. His own gardens have become
famous. They have provided a ritual for living which is expressed in
the quality of contemplation his art demanded.

In 1943, after a controversial discharge from the Army, Graves returned
to his home, "The Rock," on Fidalgo Island in Washington. *Journey,* a
picture of a chalice beached against a rocky wall on the shore, may be read
as a symbol of the artist's return. By this time it had become axiomatic
that Graves was a painter of symbols. Throughout the years, he appears
in his paintings and drawings as various creatures of the forest, as a bird,
or a fish, or a flower. His interest in Eastern thought, religions, and rituals
has contributed to this depersonalization of self into a cipher. The cup—a
containing vessel, a common object, a ceremonial implement, something
that receives and dispenses—remains in these actions itself uncontaminated
by any of its uses. Is this, then, a portrait of the artist's self?

The dark browns and umbers of this drawing are enlivened by the mystical light brought into the composition by a network of phosphorescent
white lines. This so-called "white writing" was developed by Mark Tobey
a decade earlier in England and has been utilized by many artists in the
Pacific Northwest; but none has achieved the individuality of Graves.
This linear device unifies the composition and, in wider brushstrokes,
provides highlights that define the planar aspects of the subject. By employing a light that seems to rise from within the rocks and the cup, Graves
provokes a mythic or spiritual interpretation of the drawing. The sky behind the crystalline rocks is dark, abstracted, and withholds its light.
An artist in the tradition of the Transcendentalists, Graves brings to the
fore questions about the role of the artist and his works in the life of
America today.

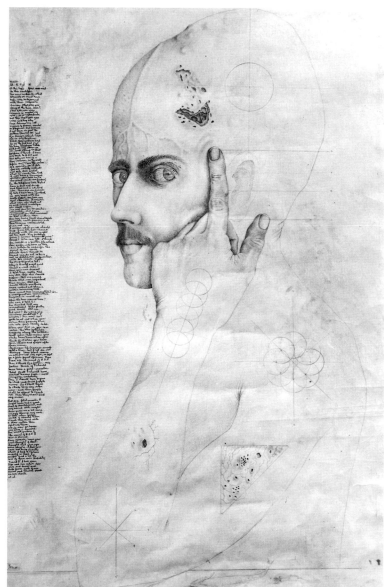

John Wilde

b. 1919

Wedding Portrait, 1943

Graphite on paper, 27¾ x 17¼
(70.5 x 43.8)

Gift of the artist in memory of
Helen Wilde   70.75

Wedding Portrait, 1943

Graphite on paper, 27¾ x 17¾
(70.5 x 45.1)

Gift of the artist in memory of
Helen Wilde   70.74

PROVENANCE

The artist

EXHIBITIONS

Whitney Museum of American Art, New
York, *American Master Drawings and
Watercolors,* 1976, p. 432 (traveled);
Montgomery Museum of Fine Arts, Ala-
bama, *American Art 1934–1956: Selections
from the Whitney Museum of American
Art,* 1978, pp. 102–03 (traveled); WMAA
1979, n.p.; Whitney Museum of American
Art, *Decade of Transition: 1940–1950,*
1981, n.p.; Elvehjem Museum of Art, Uni-
versity of Wisconsin-Madison, *John Wilde:
Drawings 1940–1984,* 1984, pp. 14–15;
WMAA 1986, n.p.

The portrait in mid-century American art has not fared well. It has fallen
to the province of often skilled commercial craftsman who are able to
produce a stylish image in a certain size for a fee. Their styles echo the
past and compete with the photograph. The matched pair of marriage
portrait drawings by John Wilde are exceptions.

In his early years, Wilde was grouped with the Magic Realists, those
artists who used considerable technical facility to depict images with an
excruciating graphic intensity and clarity, imparting to their subject matter a surreal or otherworldly feeling. Their aspirations tended to echo
past achievements such as those of the Northern printmakers or Dürer.
This meticulous realism, apparent in Wilde's two sheets, is tinged with
the darker side of the artist's fantasy. In these two undraped figures,
Wilde's obsessive observations are enlarged by the addition of texts and an
assortment of symbols. There is in each sheet a monstrous transformation
of the head, a cephalic abscess implying that the head is not only the
repository of information or intelligence, but of dreams, fantasies, and
nightmares. The mathematical formulae and charts turn the body into a
surface for intellectual graffiti. The elbow placed on the ledge echoes
the Renaissance and Baroque portrait tradition of a figure in a window.
These historical remnants are consistent in reflecting the academic world
in which Wilde has lived and taught for many decades.

The self-portrait is autobiography, with its attendant lures, traps, and
occasions for aggrandizement or self-deprecation. Wilde stresses the
profile, well defined, and an open, looser presentation of the rest of the
figure. Both pointing fingers echo the iconography of St. John the Baptist,
but his finger, pressed against the head, assumes an intellectual stress,
while his wife's, aimed at the sky, suggests a mystic openness. The proportional scale markings on his head imply an ideal balance between
man and art.

The portrait of Wilde's wife is endowed with more symbols and suggestions. A landscape with a column topped by a large bird with spread wings
is attended by a standing skeleton; further on, a dessicated tree trunk; at
left, a well or tomb surmounted by a colonnade; and, in the sky, blurred
impressions of birds in flight. Again the torso is blemished by fissures and
signs of decay. Is this a shared feature of their association? Beauty and
decay are an ancient combination and this sun-bleached landscape seems
devoid of life. Whatever the symbolism, Wilde rendered his motifs with a
carefully controlled pencil where individual marks are often blended
into brilliantly modulated tones.

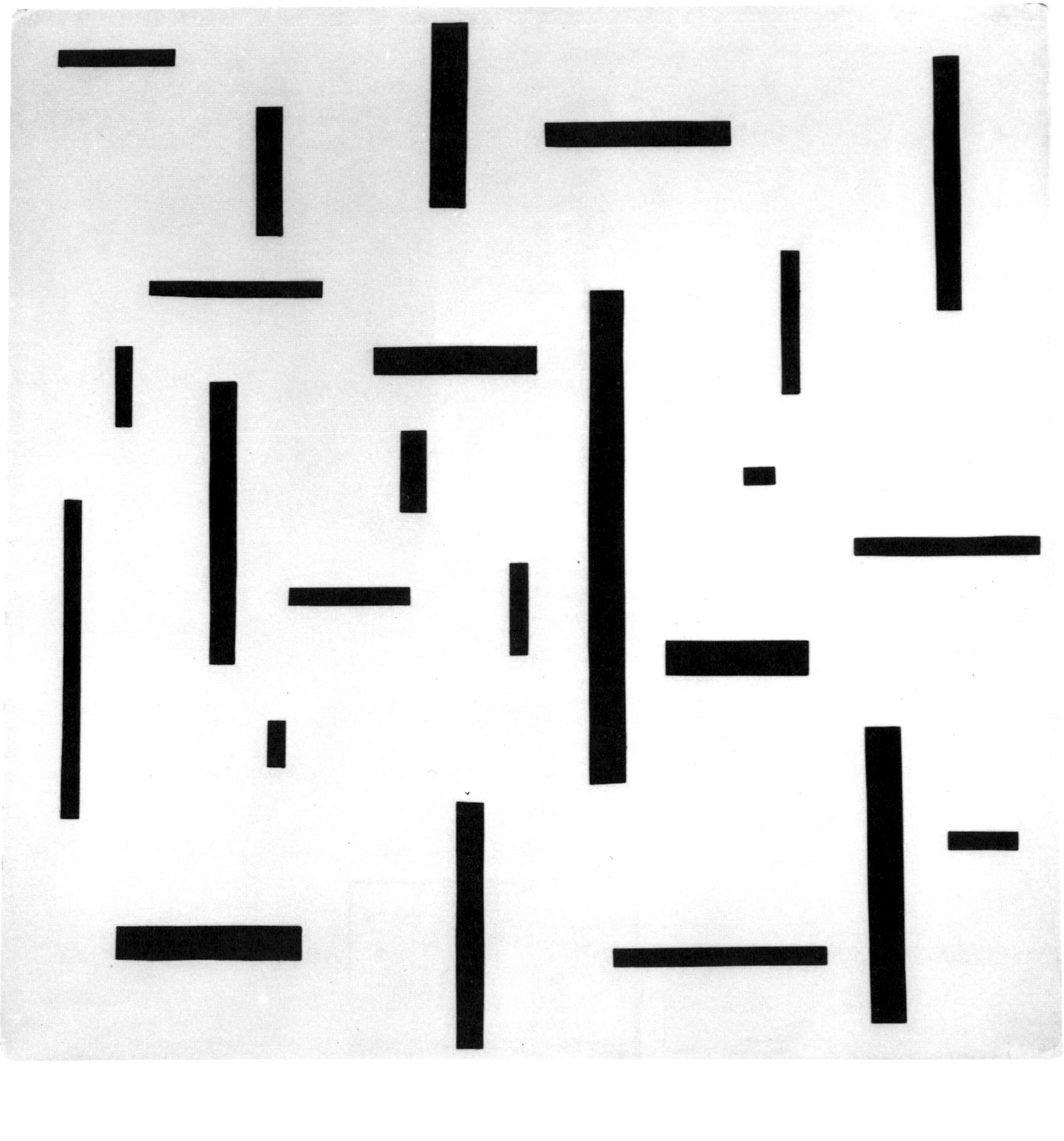

Burgoyne Diller

1906–1965

Prior to World War II, few Americans employed collage, and those who did often used found materials. Cut photographs or printed images were edited into novel arrangements, frequently under a Surrealist influence. The pure geometry of Burgoyne Diller's collages stood almost alone in the modernist art world.

Diller's geometry, produced like Mondrian's, with visual sensibility as the deciding force, required years of thought for perfection. He began slowly, using collage as a pasted element of color in small drawings. Carefully cut snips of printed or hand-colored paper were shaped as needed to fit the broad lines or planes. He came to rely upon the cut edge increasingly as he progressed to even larger works. Late in his career he drew on the canvas with charcoal and pinned on strips of colored paper in ever-changing locations as he formulated a composition. Edge becomes line. A strip of cut yellow or red paper pasted on a field of black enriches a composition, but at the same time each retains a discrete elemental aspect.

Untitled, composed of black strips of paper held in a refined visual tension on a white field, is one of Diller's largest and most accomplished collages. It is a statement unto itself, for there is no record of any painting following its exact pattern. The varying widths and lengths of the bits of paper display a modest degree of retinal play in the gray after-images which move abruptly about the page. This interplay also appears in Diller's paintings and anticipates the effect developed to an excessive degree by the Op painters two decades later. Bars of black show not only direction by their length, but argue for spatial depth and an implicit perspectival reading as they interrelate to one another. The longer bars establish compositional division, which leads to visual segmentation. Diller's art is complex, demanding sustained contemplation to reveal itself.

Untitled, 1944

Collage on board, 15 x 15 (38.1 x 38.1)

Purchase, with funds from the Mr. and Mrs. M. Anthony Fisher Purchase Fund, Martin and Agneta Gruss, and the Felicia Meyer Marsh Purchase Fund   82.21

PROVENANCE

The artist; Sylvia Pizitz; Washburn Gallery, New York

EXHIBITIONS

WMAA 1985, p. 24

Alfonso Ossorio

b. 1916

Ossorio, an exceptionally literate artist, has always revealed an extraordinary display of emotional drama in his art. This expression is achieved by complex subject matter and a graphic sensibility which informs the style of his drawing as well as his sculpture. His early work bears the influences of his multinational education—in his Philippine homeland and later England, followed by Harvard University and art school. Having been interested in calligraphy as a youth, he later sought to express himself in discrete still-life images and portraits made in the style of the Magic Realists, but with Surrealist freedoms.

During World War II, Ossorio worked in military hospitals in America, among them Camp Ellis on the Spoon River in Illinois. What he saw is reconstituted in *Red Star:* the surgeon's white rubber gloves transformed into black, the shattered bodies and limbs, the mummy of bandages, as well as the resounding explosions which inflicted such wounds. The image of the wound in art has a lengthy history, from St. Sebastian's arrow-pierced body to these contemporary images of bleeding heart valves and orifices, natural or inflicted wounds, which fill a Midwest landscape with medieval visions of terror and destruction.

Realism, transformed into meaning-charged symbols drawn without a display of virtuoso draftsmanship, demonstrates Ossorio's commitment to the substance of his message. In these early drawings, moreover, we can see the characteristic rhythmic shapes and interlockings of his later abstract paintings. Made with flowing paint in gestures which echo those of his friend Jackson Pollock, these later works continue to be enriched by Ossorio's humanistic interests. He has made a significant contribution to the modern art of mid- and late twentieth-century America.

Red Star, 1944

Watercolor and ink on paper, 13½ x 19¾
(34.3 x 50.2) sight

Gift of the artist   69.153

PROVENANCE

The artist

EXHIBITIONS

Whitney Museum of American Art, New York, *Recent Acquisitions by the Museum and Its Friends,* 1970, n.p.; WMAA 1979, n.p.; Whitney Museum of American Art, *Decade of Transition: 1940–1950,* 1981, n.p.

Jackson Pollock

1912–1956

Pollock's generation felt an extraordinary pressure to cut the ties with European traditions, a pressure expressed in a driving invention of new iconographies and techniques. It was an ambition that finally led Pollock to break the traditional figure-ground relationship and thereby establish a new pictorial unity. After the mid-1940s, he no longer used line, light, tone, and space as the basic elements of his drawing or painting. He had by this time transformed his gestures into a configuration which was *of* the picture plane and contained images elicited from the raw flux of action. The gesture remained evident in the substance of the image. Informing these swirling masses of lines and spills of paint or ink were the totemic images which evolved in his imagination from previous decades.

In *Untitled,* an abstract composition, we catch not only something of the frenzied balance of Pollock's shapes, but evidence of process invention, which was so crucial to his generation of artists. These freely brush-drawn images were later worked over in a layering process to achieve new and novel shapes. Ink tends to blend into itself, so that the layering produced only increased density. There is in this series of broken, isolated fragments a suggestion of homogeneity. The drawing can be read as if the artist were working dark into light, isolating fragments of luminous paper, which occasionally reveal areas of underdrawing. By arbitrarily painting with the brush over an initial image, in response to psychological stimulae, the artist produces new raw configurations which echo his emotional state. At the same time, these new shapes serve as the vocabulary for later paintings.

Untitled, 1944

Ink and gouache on paper, 13⅛ x 11⅛ (33.3 x 28.3)

Purchase, with funds from the Julia B. Engel Purchase Fund and the Drawing Committee   85.20

PROVENANCE

Lee Krasner Pollock Estate; Jason McCoy Inc., New York

EXHIBITIONS

WMAA 1985, p. 45

Milton Avery

1885–1965

Line drawings by Avery are usually spare, occasionally enlivened with touches of hatching. His watercolors are frequently progressions from what originally began as linear images. The addition of color, the reemphasis on the subject revisited, and Avery's direct way of working with the liquid material may all be seen in *Lone Rock and Surf*. An artist who conceived his works serially, Avery would contemplate this image again in 1953, when it served as subject for the painting *Advancing Sea*.

Painterly drawings, especially those made with a brush, have a significant tradition in American modern art. In *Lone Rock and Surf,* Avery concentrates on the portrait of an isolated rock besieged by relentless waves. While he is rarely considered a symbolist, this image could suggest steadfastness. Color is a unifying element in much of his work. The variety of brushstrokes enlivens this rather abstract image, with its busy foreground, calm distance, and corona of boiling water, which introduces light as the composition's defining factor. The high horizon projects forward more than it recedes, an effect which reduces the depth of field, thereby stressing the picture plane and, in doing so, suggests that Avery responded to similar compositional devices in Oriental prints.

Avery's delight in nature differs from the calculated distance and impersonality in the works of that other noted watercolorist, John Marin. In Avery's watercolors, brushed lines are overdrawn to enhance their surface features, adding a decorative touch. The twisting, intertwining lines in the lower portion of the composition support the weight of the great rock to provide a dramatic contrast to the relentless horizon and the distant, evenly surfaced sea. It is a delight to experience the artist's pleasure in the churning lines, in his energetic, dry-brush application. The obdurate rock, intractable in the mobile sea, is not a replication of an object, but the recording of an experience which is shared with the viewer. The variety of brushstrokes, reinforced by the color, animates the image.

Lone Rock and Surf, 1945

Watercolor on paper mounted on cardboard, 22½ x 30¼ (57.2 x 76.8)

Purchase, with funds from S. Sidney Kahn and the Drawing Committee   84.68

PROVENANCE

Milton and Sally Avery Arts Foundation, Inc., New York

EXHIBITIONS

WMAA 1985, p. 15

Arshile Gorky

1905–1948

Tragedy, that great stimulant, clung to Gorky as if he were its last friend. In January 1946, a studio fire destroyed his drawings, sketches, and books. The following month he was operated on for cancer. Nevertheless, that summer, while staying at his wife's family farm, he produced 292 drawings, of which *Drawing* is one.

These summer drawings were made out-of-doors in the lush fields of Virginia. This vernal ambiance elicited Gorky's most poetic images. In *Drawing*, the open space filled with delicate delineations reveals that while he may have begun by looking at specific objects, it was the imaginative response to nature that provoked him, not the need for reportorial rendering. The recent readings of Gorky's work which attempt to reconstruct the original sources miss the point—that the artist wished to establish a new world of images and experience. The spatial expansiveness, the thin line carefully encompassing a shape, the dark touches of pencil or color which define surface and stop the eye all revel in this new world. While it is possible, through a process of questionable mental gymnastics, to locate "realistic" images in Gorky's work, that activity is better suited to psychological perception tests. Like so many modern artists, Gorky drew to increase his vocabulary of images. Few of his later drawings became direct studies for paintings. The motifs he developed appear transformed, restated in differing contexts and frequently in brilliant color. Like Matta, Tanguy, Picasso, or Ernst, Gorky borrowed what he felt he required from tradition.

The loosely drawn biomorphic images, or the dot-formed circles connected with lines or smudges of gray are filled with suggestion. These are the images of a poetic mind turning the obvious into a novel and thrilling experience for both mind and spirit. Gorky's lyrical line encompasses shapes built from fantasies upon real objects. This imbues the shapes with a history to which the viewer responds. In the free metamorphosis that engenders these vibrant images, the landscape becomes still life or abstraction.

Drawing, 1946

Graphite and crayon on paper,
19 1/16 x 25 1/16 (48.4 x 63.7)

50th Anniversary Gift of Edith and Lloyd
Goodrich in honor of Juliana Force   82.48

PROVENANCE

Ethel K. Schwabacher, New York;
Edith and Lloyd Goodrich

EXHIBITIONS

WMAA 1981, p. 25

David Smith

1906–1965

One of the most inventive twentieth-century American draftsmen, David Smith produced drawings throughout his career for intellectual enjoyment as well as for stimulating the evolution of potential images in his sculpture. He began as a painter, but soon discovered that his true talent was to be revealed in sculpture. In this context, he drew throughout his career in diverse styles, whether in sketchbooks or small drawings recording things seen in books, galleries, or in the countryside where he lived. He would also record completed sculptures with titles, dates, weight, colors, and dimensions. Throughout most of his life he made drawings from the model; these range from sketchbook page size to large canvases. As he said, the drawings were for sculpture that would be and that would never be. Drawing became the process for rapidly expanding his vocabulary of forms and ideas.

Untitled is a synthesis of things seen and imagined. The shell shape most likely comes from the shells Smith gathered during a stay in the Virgin Islands in 1931. The pyramidal shape topped with a sphere relates to the sculpture *Billiard Player Construction* of 1937. The handlike shape emerging from the shell and holding a female figure could be a representation of the sculptor's hand molding unformed material to his needs. Like so many other American artists of this century, Smith produced many drawings with brush and ink or paint. His initial experience as a painter remained with him, finding expression in the plasticity of his sculpture.

Untitled, 1946

Tempera on paper, 22 x 30¼ (55.9 x 76.8)

Purchase, with funds from The Lauder Foundation—Drawing Fund   79.45

PROVENANCE

The artist; M. Knoedler and Co., New York

EXHIBITIONS

Whitney Museum of American Art, New York, *David Smith: The Drawings,* 1979, p. 114; Whitney Museum of American Art, *Decade of Transition: 1940–1950,* 1981, n.p.; WMAA 1981, p. 51; WMAA 1981a, n.p.; Hirshhorn Museum and Sculpture Garden, Smithsonian Institution, Washington, D.C., *David Smith: Painter, Sculpture, Draftsman,* 1983, p. 70 (traveled)

Ad Reinhardt

1913–1967

As a youth, Reinhardt copied English and German black letter printing. In college he drew cartoons with a bold graphic flair that revealed a biting satire. By his mid-twenties he was painting, and a decade later maintained a studio next door to that of Stuart Davis, another hard-minded inventive artist. During these years, Reinhardt discovered the worlds of modernism and abstraction. The evolution of his style reveals an intelligent awareness of his own achievements and a striving toward new goals. At one time he made collages by cutting photos to fragments, so that only hints of recognizable images remained. These were assembled in gridlike formations which had a strong tonal value but lacked the anecdotalism that might have occurred with such representational fragments. During the 1940s, as in this untitled sheet, he drew, with a brush, a screen of shapes possibly derived from the alphabetic forms that had previously fascinated him. Over these black constructs on white paper he painted thick strokes of color, obscuring the framework. In the ensuing years, Reinhardt eliminated the primary grid and increased the width of the brushstroke, placing each one in an orderly pattern like that of mosaic tesserae. At this point he was approaching his mature style of soft-textured, hard-edged geometric rectangles.

Reinhardt achieved a new style by obliterating the near calligraphy of his work with a system of plus and minus signs, possibly derived from his knowledge of Neo-plasticism and Mondrian. Increasingly, he chose to reduce the emotional response to gesture and color by setting forth his image in rectangles, conjoined in patterns, rejecting light, space, texture, and personal handwriting. His perverse sense of values, if not humor, uses drawing to eliminate drawing from his art. He strove to establish an art which was the end of art as art. Nevertheless, his drawings are among the most inventive and challenging of those made during the 1940s. They illustrate the old maxim that the most inventive turns of art are those which appear for the first time in the artist's drawings.

Untitled, c. 1947

Gouache on mat board, 16 x 20 (40.6 x 50.8)

50th Anniversary Gift of Rita Reinhardt
79.58

PROVENANCE

The artist; The Pace Gallery, New York

EXHIBITIONS

Whitney Museum of American Art, New York, *Decade of Transition: 1940–1950*, 1981, n.p.; Whitney Museum of American Art, *Ad Reinhardt: A Concentration from the Permanent Collection of the Whitney Museum of American Art*, 1981, p. 15; WMAA 1981, p. 39

Willem de Kooning

b. 1904

Landscape, Abstract, c. 1949

Oil on paper mounted on board,
19 x 25½ (48.3 x 64.8)

Gift of Mr. and Mrs. Alan H. Temple
68.96

PROVENANCE

The artist; Mr. and Mrs. Alan H. Temple

EXHIBITIONS

Miami-Dade Community College—South
Campus, Miami, Florida, *Abstract Expressionism: Works from the Collection of the
Whitney Museum of American Art,* 1976,
p. 8; Montgomery Museum of Fine Arts,
Alabama, *American Art 1934–1956: Selections from the Whitney Museum of American Art,* 1978, pp. 54–55; WMAA 1979,
n.p.; Whitney Museum of American Art,
New York, *Decade of Transition: 1940–
1950,* 1981, n.p.; WMAA 1982, n.p.; Whitney Museum of American Art, *Willem de
Kooning: Drawings, Paintings, Sculpture,*
1984, p. 38 (traveled)

The idea of abstraction as a form of art first arises in the writings of Balzac
and Baudelaire. Some half-century later, in 1910, Kandinsky produced the
first abstraction, a watercolor. Since that moment, many modes of abstraction have emerged. The American artists of the 1930s who chose to shift
from figurative styles into abstraction usually followed the geometrics of
the Constructivists or Neo-plastic theories. Among the few who evolved
into non-figurative painters of an expressionist tendency were Jackson
Pollock, David Smith, and de Kooning, the last especially in his drawings.
Freely painted, often brightly colored, occasionally in black and white,
these images, with their gritty textured surfaces, reveal the artist's struggle
to bring them to fruition. A linear quality also pervades these Abstract
Expressionist drawings.

De Kooning eschewed the kind of mythic symbolism buried in the images
of his friend Jackson Pollock. De Kooning's images reflected his own early
paintings, though they also echoed the accomplishments of Arshile Gorky,
the artist-friend he most admired. De Kooning's multi-referential style
became the source of the gestures he would apply to either abtract or
figurative paintings.

Landscape, Abstract is less dense in surface than is the significant series
of black-and-white paintings de Kooning made during these years, but it
has the same free expressive individuality. His poured line was reworked
with a palette knife which spread the thick paint, producing planar areas
of unplanned shape and size. A form of chance operation or automatism—
used with greater abandon by Americans than by Europeans—enriched
the opportunities for inventing new and astounding images. The free-
flowing lines are a simulacra of the creative process. Just as handwriting
reveals individuality, so the gesture of the artist reveals its creator. What
might be considered self-referential linear patterns or bold shapes may
echo things seen or heard, or dreams; they can also be experienced as
dynamic graphic marks with an independent appeal. Although de Kooning
is reluctant to comment on his art, to explain his specific thoughts during
the time he painted, his work remains, like all high abstraction, among the
most sophisticated and challenging artistic expressions in the second
half of the twentieth century.

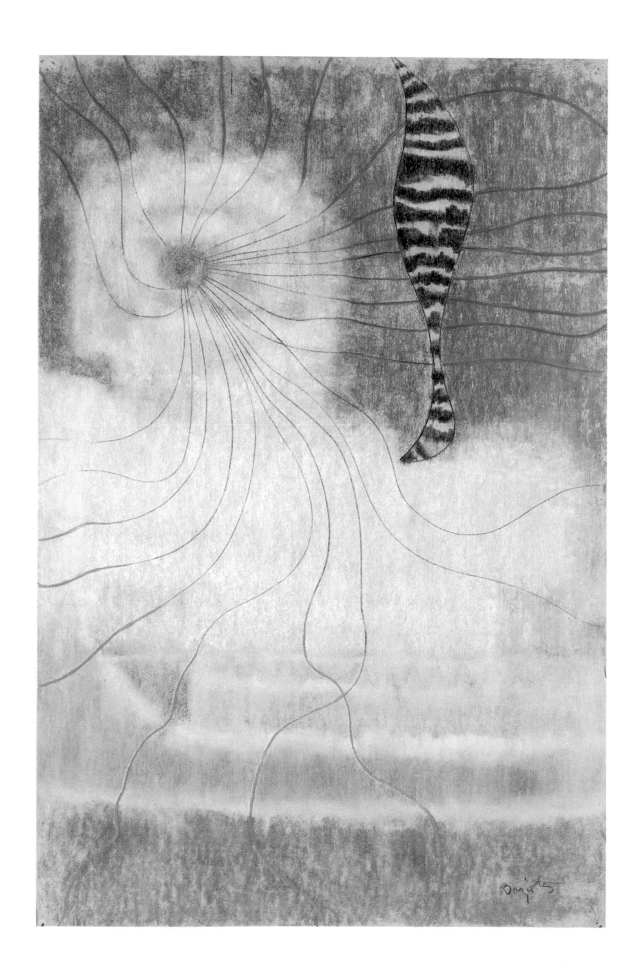

William Baziotes

1912–1963

The traditional conventions of function and skill in drawing were challenged and transformed in American art by the first generation modernists. Drawing was to become an act whose end product was not a depiction of some pre-existing imagery, but, like the accomplished painting and sculpture of the time, the expression of the process through which the form itself would emerge. Hence there was no need for a model, because the results were elicited in the making of the image.

To be inspired, possessed, obsessed, but most of all to be inspired—this is what Baziotes, as a representative of the newly emerging art, believed to be the artist's role. Art was an act of risk, necessary if one was to attain revelation. He likened himself to the prize-fighter, alert, battling, and responsive to the slightest nuance. As a youth he had worked in a stained-glass factory, and crystalline, light-capturing fragments of glass may have lingered in his mind when making pastel drawings.

Baziotes' presentation drawings are normally sustained events in themselves, with no further exploration in paintings. *Sea Forms*, with its broad planes of textured color and grained background where massed lines become surface, depicts a vortex, or eye, from which radiate a series of lines or tentacles. In this sea of liquid color a biomorphic shape descends over the striations, suggesting the intrusion of an unknown sea creature. Baziotes' transmogrified shapes are laden with the experience of sensate stimuli. These are not shapes conjured only from the mind's hallucinations, but from the contemplation of natural phenomena, which have passed through the artist's imagination. Although images are built with care and consideration, these palpating figures are not the products of abstracted intellectualization.

Sea motifs and forms appeared in the work of many American artists during the 1940s and 1950s, but few artists responded with the inventive conviction of Baziotes. What concerned him was the activity of making art. To this, all else was subservient. "It is the mysterious that I love in painting, it is the stillness and the silence. I want my pictures to take effect very slowly, to obsess and to haunt."

Sea Forms, 1951

Pastel on paper on masonite, 38⅛ x 25⅛ (96.8 x 63.8)

Purchase   52.19

PROVENANCE

The artist; Kootz Gallery, New York

EXHIBITIONS

Contemporary Arts Museum, Houston, *The Magical Worlds of Redon, Klee, Baziotes,* 1957, n.p.; Marlborough Gallery, New York, *William Baziotes: Late Work 1946–1962,* 1971, p. 13; Whitney Museum of American Art, New York, *American Master Drawings and Watercolors,* 1976, p. 349 (traveled); Whitney Museum of American Art, *Selections from the Lawrence H. Bloedel Bequest,* 1977, p. 12; Montgomery Museum of Fine Arts, Alabama, *American Art 1934–1956: Selections from the Whitney Museum of American Art,* 1978, p. 62 (traveled)

Philip Guston

1913–1980

Between 1948 and 1949, Guston traveled in Italy, studying the Old Masters. It was a moment when he did not paint. About 1950 he began a series of abstract paintings, which he continued until 1967–68. During these years he was a prolific draftsman, employing a painterly line to depict shapes that suggested still-life sources. Drawn as flat configurations, these often interlocking forms continued to exhibit a dynamism not seen in the brightly colored paintings. While his paintings relied on an appealing unctuous surface, his drawings were mostly executed in a stark manner with black ink and a brush. He is thus included in that large body of painterly draftsmen who are among the most inventive in twentieth-century American art.

Ink Drawing, an early work in his abstract series, is already filled with the rotund forms and dark bunched lines that would characterize the drawings of this period. Some pages are densely filled with lines, either cautious or writhing, while other drawings are open and skeletal in their configurations. In contrast to the early drawing for *Conspirators*, with its echoes of Old Master influence, this 1952 sheet is dramatically modern. Its linear construction is on the paper's surface and little depth is suggested or attempted. The movement of the line describes small shapes or could be read as a free gestural expression in itself. The open space and the light of the page enhance its forms while the marvelous inventiveness in each line animates the whole page. Guston, always an artist with literary inclinations, is freed from figuration and message-bearing in these abstract works. They may, however, indirectly reveal a subject matter. Abstract Expressionism opened the way for an excessive display of temperament. In Guston's form of abstraction, there seems to be a striving toward a purification of image in the demands made on each line to clarify the whole image. The playfulness in these lines, as they trail off into space, or echo each other to reinforce a shape, instills in the viewer a feeling of participation in the creative act. This intimacy is one of the most significant aspects of the best abstract painting.

Ink Drawing, 1952, 1952

Ink on paper, 18⅝ x 23⅝ (47.3 x 60)

Purchase, with funds from the Friends of the Whitney Museum of American Art
61.23

PROVENANCE

The artist; Sidney Janis Gallery, New York

EXHIBITIONS

Whitney Museum of American Art, New York, *The First Five Years: Acquisitions 1957–1962*, 1962, n.p.; University Art Museum, University of Texas, Austin, *Drawings*, 1966, p. 39; Miami-Dade Community College—South Campus, Miami, Florida, *Abstract Expressionism: Works from the Collection of the Whitney Museum of American Art*, 1976, p. 6; WMAA 1979, n.p.; WMAA 1982, n.p.

Yasuo Kuniyoshi

1889–1953

Once, for a brief time, Kuniyoshi had a job with a circus. It was to have a lasting effect on his artistic subject matter. In this late work, the last and largest of his complete drawings, he examines the juggler who, as a bitter-sweet entertainer, functions behind a mask. The mask, a symbolic element here, is used to state deep emotional comments which Kuniyoshi's Japanese nature would not allow to be expressed directly. He had suffered during World War II when as a Japanese he often fell under one form of suspicion or another; in the early 1950s he was old and ill. Concurrently, he saw the rise of Abstract Expressionism, which left him with the feeling that his own art was now out-of-date.

This bold dramatic image, formed in highlights on a page of near-total blackness, depicts the artist-juggler in performance. The paper party hat, the elongated nose, the bouncing balls, and the gloved hand are seen within the tent. Through an opening we can see the guy lines, poles, and the top branches of a tree. Kuniyoshi is unconcerned with social realism and its political overtones, and concentrates on deep personal feelings. An emotional portrait, the dramatic design with its hard content often produced an uneasy response from many viewers. *Juggler* is certainly as forceful as any of the best of the German Expressionist works. Its emotional impact is enhanced by the artist's use of a dense, confined composition. The gritty texture which defines the mask is in sharp contrast to the firm design and the elegant, smooth surfaces.

Juggler, 1952

Ink on cardboard, 22 x 28 (55.9 x 71.1) sight

Purchase   53.37

PROVENANCE

The artist; The Downtown Gallery, New York

EXHIBITIONS

The Downtown Gallery, New York, *Kuniyoshi's Circus Pictures*, 1955; Milwaukee Junior League, *An Exhibition of Circus Subjects*, 1955; Currier Gallery of Art, Manchester, New Hampshire, *Exhibition of Contemporary American Drawings*, 1956; Hofstra College, Fine Arts Department, Hempstead, New York, *Art and the Theater*, 1957; Contemporary Arts Museum, Houston, *Exhibition of Contemporary Drawings*, 1958; University Gallery, University of Florida, *Yasuo Kuniyoshi*, 1969, no. 83 (traveled); John and Mable Ringling Museum of Art, Sarasota, Florida, *The Circus in Art*, 1977, n.p. (traveled); WMAA 1979, n.p.; WMAA 1986, n.p.

David Smith

1906–1965

In his drive toward what would become a form of emblematic abstraction, especially in his drawings, Smith would allow images to unfold from his subconscious imagination in vague shapes that he could then edit into definition. This can be observed in such sheets as *Eng No. 6,* which is constructed of a mass of endless, moving lines. These inchoate gestures are defined by painting in, that is, by boldly editing the edges, forcing a defined central image. This image is a biomorphic accumulation of fragments of other images, similar to shapes which appear years later in various sculptures. Even in these large presentation drawings, Smith did not draw with a specific sculpture in mind. Rather, he was manipulating experienced shapes to merge into newly discovered configurations, which might or might not emerge later in the sculptures. That Smith had feminine attributes in mind for most of his sculptures—he claimed that he made only "girl" sculptures—is revealed in their round, sensual shapes replete with arcs, curves, and indentations. His fecundity is nowhere as excitingly revealed as in the variety of dynamic impulses which engender his drawings.

A brush can quickly cover large areas, and the painting-in process is encouraged by this efficiency. The process allowed Smith to create protuberances, increasing the fiordlike inroads toward the center. The results also increase the dynamics of the negative space. The refinements of Smith's hand in drawing were directed toward the making of an image. He was not given to forming a refined hand with which to "draw" images. The swiftly moving gestures in these painterly drawings engage the eye, while revealing the substance of his imagination.

Eng No. 6, 1952

Tempera and oil on paper, 29¾ x 42¼ (75.6 x 107.3)

Purchase, with funds from Mrs. Agnes Gund and the H. van Ameringen Foundation   79.43

PROVENANCE

Estate of the artist; M. Knoedler and Co., New York

EXHIBITIONS

Whitney Museum of American Art, New York, *David Smith: The Drawings*, 1979, p. 53; WMAA 1981, p. 51; WMAA 1981a, n.p.; WMAA 1982, n.p.; Whitney Museum of American Art at Philip Morris, New York, *Twentieth-Century Sculpture: Process and Presence*, 1983, p. 15

Richard Lindner

1901–1978

Richard Lindner arrived in the United States from Germany in 1941, at age forty-one, to commence a career as a commercial artist. It was only in the early 1950s that he seriously turned his labors to the fine arts. Chronologically, then, *Sunday Afternoon* of 1954 is an early work. In a painting of the previous year, entitled *The Meeting*, Lindner portrayed himself as a child in a sailor suit. He appears in this guise again in *Sunday Afternoon*, in a continuing examination of his childhood.

A collector of toys and dolls, Lindner frequently turned his painted figures into marionettes and puppets. The consequent dehumanizing is apparent in the implied psychological distance between the characters in this drawing. Lindner's mother was an American, and yet he straddled European and American culture, using the experience of his youth to comment on life as he found it in New York. Women remained a preoccupation. His mature images reveal them transformed from the romantic, though distracted, charming figure in this family portrait, into monsters of high polychromed vulgarity.

A self-described literary artist, Lindner reveled in a theatrical display of anecdote and content. In this drawing, with its modern, spare, bold forms, there remain areas of mystery defined by tonal modeling. Graphic devices combine to insinuate, while still camouflaging, aspects of the artist's intent. The lightly drawn lines which initially describe shapes and areas are overworked with darker lines to render the specificity of the forms. The refinement of details distracts our eye from the overall composition, losing it in the study of minute areas.

Sunday Afternoon, 1954

Graphite and watercolor on paper,
25 x 19 (63.5 x 48.3)

Purchase, with funds from the Friends of
the Whitney Museum of American Art
60.3

PROVENANCE

The artist; Betty Parsons Gallery,
New York

EXHIBITIONS

Städische Kunsthalle Düsseldorf, West
Germany, *Richard Lindner*, 1974, no. 45
(traveled); Museum of Contemporary Art,
Chicago, *Richard Lindner: A Retrospective
Exhibition*, 1977, p. 27; WMAA 1979, n.p.;
WMAA 1986, n.p.

Theodore Roszak

1907–1981

During the years he was producing Constructivist sculpture, Roszak had abandoned figural references but, following World War II, he began a series of drawings that reveal an apocalyptic vision of the world. These often large sheets were covered with swirling lines depicting planets in collision, monstrous birds of prey in flight, and musings on the collapse of the world as we know it. Tree roots, fish carcasses, insects, jetsam and seashore refuse were combined into complex, sometimes mystifying structures frequently imbued with insistent horror.

Visionary drawings such as *Star Burst* did not find direct expression in sculpture. These monumental pages functioned as manifestations of his imagination and of his interest in the sciences as they influenced man and the world. As the imaginative writings of H. G. Wells inspired visions of the atomic bomb, so Roszak seems to be illustrating for us the final war of the worlds.

These late drawings are a fascinating, obsessive examination of momentary explosions, depicted with a profusion of lines augmented by the building up of areas with a tonal wash. The pen, often considered an implement of delicate, intimate expression, is used here in the making of monumentally scaled images. The sweep of the line is astounding in its efficient control and dramatic depictions. An ability to render small areas to be read at a short distance, but which combine to form larger elements easily read at a great distance, is a rare occurrence in the history of drawing. These ruptured baroque shapes are comparable to the claw shapes appearing in Roszak's sculpture. The composition is contained and formally structured on the page, with a smaller echo of the main image at upper left, which encourages suggestions of interstellar space. Roszak exemplifies the point that many of the best American artists do not represent a specific school of artistic endeavor, but function in individual isolation.

Star Burst, 1954

India ink and colored ink on paper,
43½ x 79 (110.5 x 200.7)

Gift of Mrs. Theodore Roszak   83.33.10

PROVENANCE

The artist; Mrs. Theodore Roszak, New York

EXHIBITIONS

Whitney Museum of American Art, New York, *The Theodore Roszak Bequest,* 1984, n.p.; WMAA 1985, p. 52

Kay Sage

1898–1963

Modern drawing is not always limited by the use of traditional implements such as pens, brushes, pencils, charcoal, pastel, or crayon. The cutting edge of the scissors is often used to make the required harsh mechanical line. In the construction of this menhir, Sage has employed decalcomania, a monotype process, to create watercolored, textured pieces of paper. From these she has cut shapes, arranged the structure, and later introduced shadows by the application of additional watercolor, which also serves to unify the composition. By cutting, rather than drawing the elements, she has established a physical individuality for each of them. This is an assembled drawing, cut, pasted, and augmented by painted refinements.

A sense of uncomfortable mystery pervades the sheet. The image of a construction placed under a sullen sky, in a landscape void of references save those of an endless desert, echoes the art of Sage's husband, Yves Tanguy. The enigma of this sentinel standing in isolation is augmented by the dark shadowy tonality of its atmosphere. An air of oppressive mystery issues from this fragmented though balanced object, situated beneath a sky punctuated only by tiny spheres that imply distant asteroids, planets, or cold dead stars. The landscape is illuminated by a dessicated light that has absorbed all life from the surroundings. Yet who has passed this way, who constructed this pylon? Surrealism's mystery is one of its perpetual fascinations and most discomforting qualities. It persists as a nagging expression of the psychological importunings of man's threatening unknown spirit.

Constant Variation, 1958

Watercolor and collage on paper,
19⅛ x 26½ (48.6 x 67.3)

Gift of Flora Whitney Miller   86.71

PROVENANCE

The artist; Flora Whitney Miller

EXHIBITIONS

WMAA 1978, p. 54; WMAA 1979, n.p.;
Joseph Seagrams and Sons, New York,
Dreams and Fantasies, 1981

Robert Rauschenberg

b. 1925

A significant activity in the study of drawings is the recognition, definition, and description of the artist's mark-making methods, which reveal his hand. Among modern draftsmen, Rauschenberg is a strange exception because many of his marks seem to be impersonal. Rather than draw something, he constructs a painterly abstract image by a method which resembles collage. He elicits "realistic" images by dampening pictorial images with a solvent and rubbing over the paper with a pen, pencil, or other device, thereby transferring the image to the drawing. In this process Rauschenberg uses a dense scribble that creates a condensed rolling hatch. This fairly anonymous technique is embellished by the addition of short, brittle pencil lines or lyrical touches of gouache.

Rauschenberg's generation of artists reacted against the complexities and high abstraction of the Abstract Expressionists. Seeking a new artistic identity, they returned to figural sources, but brought with them the gestural facture of the abstract painters. Rauschenberg's geometrical structuring might have been absorbed from Josef Albers, with whom he studied at Black Mountain College in the late 1940s. Whether Rauschenberg's images are abstract or are three-dimensional found objects, Albers' geometry allows them to coalesce into defined compositions.

Photo images such as the 1958 *Untitled* may read as abstract panels of color and texture or as obscured, symbolic anecdotes that challenge interpretation. If taken as abstractions, they stress the formal principles of a surface of massed, dense gestures, imaginative plays of color, and of a carefully structured design. Whatever one's reading of them, Rauschenberg's drawings present an assortment of views of the world, seen through the transferred images, which are as impressive in their scope as they are sensitive to delicate color relationships. Rauschenberg's brittle, gritty linear additions suggest Cy Twombly's drawings more than those of any other contemporary artist. Twombly also employs the open field in his compositions, with occasional glyphs or words held in precarious balance. In comparing the drawings of the two artists, Twombly has the most identifiable hand, while Rauschenberg camouflages almost all aspects of his own.

Untitled, c. 1958

Graphite, watercolor, and magazine transfer on paper, 22¼ x 36⅛ (56.5 x 91.8)

Gift of Mr. and Mrs. B. H. Friedman   72.2

PROVENANCE

The artist; Mr. and Mrs. B. H. Friedman

EXHIBITIONS

Kennedy Galleries, New York, *The Art Students League of New York: 1875–1975,* 1975, pp. 192–93; National Collection of Fine Arts, Smithsonian Institution, Washington, D.C., *The Object as Poet,* 1976, p. 78 (traveled); Whitney Museum of American Art, New York, *200 Years of American Sculpture,* 1976, p. 210

Charles Burchfield

1893–1967

Burchfield's *Golden Dream*, a late work of 1959, reveals the denouement of his theories and accomplishments—his lifelong fascination with music as a means of augmenting his own intense experience of nature. Nature is alive with vivid color caught in a brilliant light and charged with Burchfield's visual equivalents for sound. There exists a modest tradition of sound imagery in modern painting, stemming from the Futurists and continuing today in the work of the Concrete poets and others. In the journals he kept between 1912 and 1919, Burchfield made references to sound and he soon developed a series of nearly twenty visual equivalents for specific sounds and emotions. These he employed throughout his career to express fear, elation, sadness, etc.

Some four decades after he made *Noontide in Late May*, Burchfield retains his simple, direct working methods. Pencil drawing establishes the image, which is then enhanced and completed by the incorporation of color. In the early years, his pictures contained bright colors; he then passed through a phase of employing a darkly colored palette; but late in life, the brilliantly illuminated color seen in *Golden Dream* reemerges. Burchfield's vision of nature was shaped in isolation. He never fell in with the Regionalist group during the 1930s, which kept him from imbuing his art with social problems and political harangues. He rarely visited New York or other cities and never ventured to Europe. Concerned with an art that reflected his inner life, he only rarely seems involved with modern critical approaches. Trees and plants become spectacular specimens whose transformed shapes acquire expressive form. Burchfield's type of expressionism differs from that of Northern European modernists, being couched in flowing curves and arcs rather than in their jagged, roughly brushed and often acid-toned colors.

Golden Dream portrays a single tree, transcendent, bedecked with scintillating butterflies, standing in a field before distant copes of trees. Burchfield worked out-of-doors, returning again and again to the special locations he found rewarding. By mid-life he had become a significant representative of the transcendental spirit in the twentieth century. How different his art is from the detachment shown in the work of his friend Edward Hopper, or the modern abstracting of Arthur Dove, another artist who remained isolated from the metropolis. Among the artists who examined the American world, Burchfield found a living, dynamic, individual form of expression.

Golden Dream, 1959

Watercolor on paper, 31¾ x 38
(80.6 x 96.5) sight

Promised 50th Anniversary Gift of
Mrs. Nicholas Millhouse   P.11.80

PROVENANCE

Mr. and Mrs. James N. Goodman;
Mrs. Barbara Lassiter; Mrs. Nicholas
Millhouse

EXHIBITIONS

Whitney Museum of American Art, New
York, *Charles Burchfield: A Concentration
of Works from the Permanent Collection of
the Whitney Museum of American Art,*
1980, p. 29; Whitney Museum of American
Art, *50th Anniversary Gifts,* 1980; WMAA
1981, p. 15

Franz Kline

1910–1962

For most of his life, Franz Kline painted views of New York City or the countryside of his birthplace, Pennsylvania. Few of these paintings suggest the great invention of his late abstractions. The early works lack significant individual style, and it was only in 1949, at the suggestion of Willem de Kooning, that Kline employed an opaque projector to enlarge a tiny drawing of a chair, a process that lead him into abstraction. Since the mid-1940s he had been making a series of figure studies and studio interiors delineated in a flowing brush line. These were concerned more with structure than with the presentation of the subject. The mature abstractions emerged after 1949; *Untitled* is a late work of 1960, completed two years before Kline's death at the age of fifty-two.

Kline soon realized that he could produce many compositions for paintings with his brush-drawing method and the opaque projector. Paper was often in short supply and dozens of these ink drawings were made on telephone-book yellow pages. Any decision to enlarge a drawing into a painting came after prolonged study. Kline had the rare ability to maintain the energy and inventive integrity of the drawing in the enlarged image. Soon his drawings evolved from imaginative exercises to engagements that presented the gesture itself as the subject. While the gesture may suggest to some sources in Oriental calligraphy, Kline's line actually evolved from his own drawing process, not from a form of written language.

The best of Kline's drawings are in black and white; those where he attempted to incorporate color seem to lack the inventive dynamism and control of the black-and-white sheets. *Untitled*, a design as concerned with negative as with positive space, employs triangulations and bars of thrusting lines for its animation. The horizontal bar across the top of the composition contains the image on the page, while the structure below it is an energetic abstraction. As in the drawings of Paul Klee, the gesture, with its display of pure form, carries the message.

Untitled, 1960

Ink on paper, 8½ x 10½ (21.6 x 26.7)

Purchase, with funds from Mr. and Mrs. Benjamin Weiss   78.53

PROVENANCE

The artist; Allan Stone Gallery, New York

EXHIBITIONS

WMAA 1978, p. 38; WMAA 1979, n.p.; WMAA 1982, n.p.

David Smith

1906–1965

Nature was an ever present source of graphic ideas for Smith's sculpture as well as for his drawings. He found designs in the flight patterns of birds and in the animal and bird skeletons lying on the rough hill-country farm where he lived in upstate New York. He also studied other cultures through a large library of books, annotating images and texts as he did so. *Untitled, II*, made during the high years of Abstract Expressionism, can be seen as a competitive commentary on the works of artists of his own generation. Gone is the flowing line of the Abstract Expressionist, replaced by a growing need for rigid structure. This is also apparent in Smith's sculptures, such as the Tanktotems, the Voltri and the Cubi series, which were fashioned from industrially manufactured shapes he either had made to order or adapted to his needs.

Smith drew standing up at a table before windows, surrounded by ink, brushes, paint, watercolor, and a stack of paper. As he completed a page he would drop it to the floor so that by the end of a session the floor would be carpeted with newly made wet drawings. Many of Smith's late drawings, among them *Untitled, II*, were painted with a mixture of egg yolk and India ink, which produced a viscous liquid that held the texture of the brushstroke when it was applied to the page. His new structuring ideas also inform *Untitled, II;* while there is a sense of landscape, this could easily be the product of Smith's observations on the quality of the individual brushstroke that forms the tessera in the design.

Untitled, II, 1961

India ink, egg yolk, and watercolor on paper, 25½ x 39¼ (64.8 x 99.7)

Gift of Candida Smith   62.21

PROVENANCE

The artist; Candida Smith

EXHIBITIONS

Whitney Museum of American Art, New York, *American Master Drawings and Watercolors*, 1976, p. 359 (traveled); WMAA 1979, n.p.

Ellsworth Kelly

b. 1923

For many years Ellsworth Kelly has depicted plants in his elegant linear drawings. It is in these spare studies that we discover many of his thought processes and the sources for the configurations that appear in his paintings and sculpture. In their painted redefinitions, the shapes often become more abstracted and refined, thus concealing their original source in nature. It is not the particular plant configuration that interests Kelly, but spatial effects, color, proportion, and scale. The delicate balance he achieves with these elements empowers the painted forms. Line, in an early drawing such as *Briar*, defines edges, thereby establishing the leaves' flat plan on the equally flat picture plane. A cursory examination might suggest that the weight of the line remains the same, but in fact the speed of application changes, the pencil twists and turns as the line changes direction, and varying amounts of graphite are applied to the page. These and other subtle alterations in tone and coloristic weight engage our eye. Proportion and balance can be studied in the shapes of individual leaves and in the negative and positive space of leaf and background.

Simplicity is the boldest of revelations, because it avoids the visual activity which in complex compositions can hide a myriad of problems. A spare drawing such as this, from nature, stands as an antecedent to the Minimalist aesthetic of the later 1960s.

Briar, 1963

Graphite on paper, 22⅜ x 28⅜ (56.8 x 72.1)

Purchase, with funds from the Neysa McMein Purchase Award   65.42

PROVENANCE

The artist

EXHIBITIONS

Whitney Museum of American Art, New York, *Neysa McMein Purchase Awards 1956–1966,* 1966; Whitney Museum of American Art, Downtown Branch, New York, *Nine Artists/Coenties Slip,* 1974, n.p.; Whitney Museum of American Art, *200 Years of American Sculpture,* 1976, p. 341; WMAA 1979, n.p.; WMAA 1983, n.p.; WMAA 1984, n.p.; Nassau County Museum of Fine Art, Roslyn, New York, *The House and Garden: Tenth Anniversary Exhibition,* 1986, cover

Walter Murch

1907–1967

A Canadian by birth, Murch lived in New York from the late 1920s on. He studied with Arshile Gorky and at the Art Students League and worked as a commercial artist during the Depression years. He later produced covers for magazines such as *Scientific American*. The precision instruments and equipment depicted on those covers served brilliantly as his natural choice of subject matter in the still-life mode. They might well have reminded him of the elegant and refined items sold in his father's Toronto jewelry store.

Murch usually made studies for his paintings, though few reached the elaborate presentation quality of this sheet. Working at night so as to avoid the noise of the city, he would focus a single strong light on the objects he painted or drew. The curved, metallic surfaces of these objects not only reflected the light directly, but then re-reflected it so as to multiply the sources of light. This crosslighting introduces an atmospheric quality that softens the forms. Murch came to like working on abraided, gritty surfaces. He would frequently begin painting over an old canvas acquired in a thrift shop. The objects Murch selected were usually found or bought. Occasionally a friend would give him an object that seemed appropriate. Joseph Cornell often lent him objects, retrieving them once they had been used in a picture.

Murch falls into the category of the painterly draftsman. He works over the splotchy surface in this drawing with thin hard-ruled lines which define edges against the soft smudgings that establish the object's surface. The mottled surface is arbitrarily added at some point in the process. In contrast is the care lavished on the smallest areas of the objects. The horizontal lines produce a feeling of ease and well-being, while the fullness of the other shapes reveals a sense of inviting warmth and luxury.

Study for **"The Birthday,"** 1963

Graphite, wash, and crayon on paper,
23 x 17½ (58.4 x 44.5) sight

Purchase, with funds from the Neysa
McMein Purchase Award   64.6

PROVENANCE

The artist; Betty Parsons Gallery,
New York

EXHIBITIONS

Whitney Museum of American Art, New York, *American Master Drawings and Watercolors*, 1976, p. 392 (traveled); Whitney Museum of American Art, *Selections from the Lawrence H. Bloedel Bequest*, 1977, p. 35; The Montclair Art Museum, Montclair, New Jersey, *The Alchemy of Walter Murch*, 1978; WMAA 1979, n.p.

Cy Twombly

b. 1929

What usually strikes one first about Twombly's art is that, whether drawing or painting, it is about writing—it derives from the Western writing gesture, and often includes words, sketches, or graffitilike accumulations. This closeness to writing brings one easily into his graphic expression, even if the subject matter is charged with scatological references, because such marks establish intimacy with the artist's spirit and sensibility.

In *Untitled,* Twombly catalogues, as he often does, a diary of signs, objects, lists, numbers, and reminders—a catalogue of shapes that appear in his work. There are none of the traditional ambitions of drawing, such as fine craftsmanship, though his is certainly, in modern terms, individual and accomplished. Nor is there concern for drawing pre-existing objects, for his subject matter is arrived at by observation, reading, and the transformation into glyphs. Twombly's overall designs are fields of action that seem to move easily off the page, with no limit to their potential. His drawing language has a physical presence in all its forms.

Twombly negates the suggested elegance of his gestures through a frenetic layering of lines and bunched hatching that results in a neurotic scribble. There is little reference to older drawing traditions, save to those found in public bath houses and other bawdy environments. Yet in the line there is a sense of speed, of ejection, of controlled frenzy, of priapic fertility. Many of his shapes exude sexual innuendo as they skitter and move across the page. One may agree or disagree with Twombly's vocabulary and technique, but drawings such as this engage us with their rigor of conviction and execution.

Untitled, 1964

Graphite, colored pencil, and crayon on paper, 27½ x 39⅜ (69.9 x 100)

Purchase, with funds from the Drawing Committee   84.21

PROVENANCE

Stephen Mazoh and Co., New York

EXHIBITIONS

Museum of Fine Arts, Boston, *10 Painters and Sculptors Draw,* 1984, no. 10; WMAA 1985, p. 61

Lucas Samaras

b. 1936

The impulse to draw finds its release in our times in procedures which differ from those previously found in art. Once it was incumbent upon the young studio apprentice to learn the style of his master. Later it became the rule to follow the academic rote by drawing from plaster casts, producing an articulated smooth tonal surface to form the image. Drawing, long considered as the initiating sketch of the image, has in recent times become an increasingly independent form of expression.

It would be difficult to find a precedent for an X-ray view of the artist's skull as a fit subject for portraiture, since a skull is far less individual than are facial features. While poets have conjured images of themselves in other states of being, few visual artists have attempted anything as radical as has Samaras. He is an artist of indubitable curiosity in his examination of history, himself, and the world about us.

In *Large Drawing No. 39,* Samaras reveals a strong, natural graphic sensibility. To see things unseen, to examine the future today through the accretion of knowledge and experience are characteristics that enliven his art. Double skulls, one hotly polychromed, the other in severe black, are placed on a tiled floor that reflects Samaras' interest in Byzantine art. The ritualistic obsessive gesture which describes each tile holds down the haunting image. The general surreal ambiance of this drawing, with its flat profiles, airless space, and emotional use of color elicits a strong response.

Large Drawing No. 39, 1966

Colored pencil and graphite on paper,
16¾ x 14 (42.6 x 35.6)

Gift of Howard and Jean Lipman   80.37.2

PROVENANCE

The artist; Howard and Jean Lipman

EXHIBITIONS

Whitney Museum of American Art, New York, *American Sculpture: Gifts of Howard and Jean Lipman*, 1980, n. p.; WMAA 1981, p. 47; WMAA 1981a, n.p.; WMAA 1986, n.p.

Michael Heizer

b. 1944

In the 1960s there emerged several young artists who espoused the idea of using the planet earth as raw material for art. Robert Smithson, Walter De Maria, and Michael Heizer are among the major contributors to this school through their work and writings. Because scale models could be impractical and out of place, most of the projects devised by these artists were presented initially as drawings or collages. Hemispheres, cubes, straight lines, and other fundamental geometric shapes comprise the vocabulary in this mode of sculptural expression. Whether the shapes were cut in snow, carved out of a mountainside or set into the surface of the desert, these designs were conceived to be of massive size. How large is the scale of such work when it can be truly seen only from outer space? What do these aggressive incursions into the very surface of the planet reveal? The major features discussed in describing these earthworks usually tend to be displacement, bulk, tonnage, laborers, trucks, dynamite, and the process.

In *Untitled*, an early essay into earthwork art, Heizer uses collage and painterly drawing to show a reassessment of the Meteor Crater in Winslow, Arizona. Heizer's thesis is to restate the formation of this naturally circular phenomenon into a rectangle. Carefully following the elements at this specific site, he reconstitutes the configuration, complete with the existing roadways, in his proposal. Combining an aerial photograph with his own markings, Heizer redraws in careful light and shadow the huge original, which is six hundred feet deep and four thousand feet in diameter. The working drawing suggests that the next step should be a survey of the site and the development of blueprints. Heizer's monumental concept is stated in carefully brushed surfaces. Although the earthwork was never actualized, this drawing remains one of the artist's most succinct images and presages many of his later motifs.

Untitled, 1969

Photograph, graphite, and watercolor on paper, 39 x 30 (99.1 x 76.2)

Gift of Norman Dubrow   80.26.1

PROVENANCE

The artist; Rolf Ricke; Norman Dubrow

EXHIBITIONS

WMAA 1979, n.p.; WMAA 1981, p. 27; WMAA 1981a, n.p.; WMAA 1983, n.p.

E. Ruscha   '70

Edward Ruscha

b. 1937

Still life, architecture, or sign, what is it that Ruscha offers us in this drawing? What is the portent or content of these letters? Is the pictograph an enigmatic sign of our times? In 1957, Ruscha saw Jasper Johns' *Target with Four Faces*, which, he has stated, fashioned his own artistic direction. The painting resolved his problems with surface, edge, and subject matter. Thereafter followed his deadpan depictions of strip architecture, buildings afire, and words singly or in phrases, painted or drawn in flat unmodulated surfaces. The word images were apparently without overt content and became occasions for the investigation of different typefaces, suggesting that letter style affects our response to the message. Ruscha has referred to words as "objects." He admires the photographs of Walker Evans, whose silvery luminous light and geometric designs can also be considered an influence.

Motor, a delicately colored drawing made with pencil and gunpowder as the toning agent, offers an image spread over the page without a specific suggestion as to its scale. There is no internal or external reference to the size of these letters. Is this a modest-sized tabletop arrangement or are these billboard scale, astride a sprawling desert space? That we can see inside the O's suggests either that they are small or that we have some privileged high point from which to view them. The dark opening in the O's hints at some ominous void below the smooth surface. The word *motor* implies an energy source which moves materials, machines or man, yet it is shown here as a thin, nearly substanceless surface caught in a gray light that illuminates its planes. While the use of words has a long history in modern art, Ruscha here has combined the ordinariness of a Pop art subject with an impersonal Minimalist drawing technique that adds a certain Surreal humor to the enigmatic statement.

Motor, 1970

Graphite and gunpowder on paper,
23 x 29 (58.4 x 73.7)

Purchase, with funds from The Lauder Foundation—Drawing Fund   77.78

PROVENANCE

The artist; Stephen Mazoh and Co., New York

EXHIBITIONS

WMAA 1978, p. 54; Whitney Museum of American Art, New York, *The Decade in Transition: Selections from the 1970s,* 1979, n.p.; WMAA 1979, n.p.; San Francisco Museum of Modern Art, *The Works of Edward Ruscha*, 1982, p. 79 (traveled)

Lake Union, Seattle, Wash. CO. 1972

Claes Oldenburg

b. 1929

The art of Oldenburg is often one of seeming contradiction. Images initially selected from street scenes where one might expect a gritty expressionistic style are drawn in a romantic lyrical line. Monumental architectural proposals executed in finely wrought linear compositions are frequently enlivened with delicate painterly watercolor.

Proposal for a Cathedral in the Form of a Colossal Faucet, Lake Union, Seattle is a fantasy of an incomplete church structure that stands overlooking the waterway. Oldenburg acknowledges the influences of eighteenth-century French fantasy architects, who often conceived of buildings as mythic symbols. One does not have to know the anecdotal details of Oldenburg's monumental proposals to enjoy them. The fact that this building is based on a common domestic plumbing product, aggrandized to huge proportions, is a useful bit of information, but not necessary for an effective experience of the work as a drawing.

Oldenburg's spare, elegant, mechanical drawing is augmented by hand-drawn lines, reinforced by a felicitous use of watercolor, which enhances the airy spatial ambiance of the image. Carefully worked out perspective thrusts the monument into the sky, with its thick "arms" reaching in four directions. In contrast is the freely drawn landscape and the noisy foam at the base of the falling water.

There is a sense of humor in this oversized image, but the control evident in its making reveals a thoughtful conception. Humor is often a questionable asset in a work of art, but here the brilliance of the drawing and the sharpness of concept sustain our interest. Like the Tiepolos, Oldenburg is capable of the most acute use of line and wash to suggest form and space.

Proposal for a Cathedral in the Form of a Colossal Faucet, Lake Union, Seattle, 1972

Watercolor, graphite, and colored pencil on paper, 29 x 22⅞ (73.7 x 58.1)

Purchase, with funds from Knoll International 80.35

PROVENANCE

The artist

EXHIBITIONS

WMAA 1981, p. 37; WMAA 1981a, n.p.; WMAA 1983, n.p.; Whitney Museum of American Art at Philip Morris, New York, *Twentieth-Century Sculpture: Process and Presence*, 1983, p. 27

Alexander Calder

1898–1976

Calder began as a painter, and his early ink drawings were of animals, seen either at the circus or the zoo; later, he drew spare, abstract linear compositions. The abstractions began after he visited Mondrian and were developed during his residence in Paris. His invention of the mobile freed sculpture from its traditional frozen position by introducing kinetic possibilities. The free-swinging shapes of the mobiles soon came to populate his drawings. Calder had a sense of gruff fun, partly expressed in shapes derived from those of his friend Miró. Yet his drawings also have a very practical aspect. Like David Smith, he drew for the stimulus and the rewards of invention. The play of shapes dances in this image. Few of his drawings relate to specific sculptures; rather, drawing was an arena for developing the novel forms which would find a place in his celestial kinetic world.

Calder often drew with a brush, producing the bold forms seen in *Four Black Dots*. His basic vocabulary of red, black, blue, and white is that of the Constructivists. Space is inferred by the open panels within the large central configuration and the area occupied by the dots. The patterned background on the right provides a base from which the other elements seem to move. Balance is always a significant aspect of Calder's works, and here it may be experienced in the radiating lines from the central, cloverlike motif. These parallel lines, which twist and turn, appear throughout his work, including his jewelry and kitchen utensils, and derive from sources in African trading stuffs. The swelling lines inaugurate a sense of motion or radiating energy that enthusiastically proclaims the rewards of fun and enjoyment.

Four Black Dots, 1974

Gouache on paper, 29½ x 43 (74.9 x 109.2)

Purchase, with funds from the Howard and Jean Lipman Foundation, Inc.   74.94

PROVENANCE

The artist; Perls Gallery, New York

EXHIBITIONS

Whitney Museum of American Art, New York, *Calder's Universe,* 1976, p. 123 (traveled); WMAA 1978, p. 21; Whitney Museum of American Art, *Alexander Calder: A Concentration of Works from the Permanent Collection*, 1981, p. 28; WMAA 1982, n.p.; Whitney Museum of American Art at Philip Morris, New York, *Calder: Selections from the Permanent Collection of the Whitney Museum of American Art,* 1984, p. 8

Willem de Kooning

b. 1904

All great drawings instill unquestioned believability in the viewer, a feat achieved through a statement made by a sure, skilled hand. In this de Kooning excels.

The linear demarcations in this drawing find their origins in *Manikins* or *Landscape, Abstract* of 1949. The secure gesture curves into a suggestive shape, which here represents a female figure. In the 1949 sheet, the shapes are a field of abstractions, but they echo palpable flesh. De Kooning's treatment of the figure not as a three-dimensional object, but as a source for flat, interlocking shapes recalls the aesthetic of transparency and layering that prevailed during the teens and twenties. The awkward legs, oversized shoes, the twist at midsection as indicated by the horizontal line, these give the figure a dynamic, impossible to achieve reality. A grasping hand, the lowered squinty eye, and floppy hair reveal not the reserve of a classicist, but the flailing passions of the expressionist. The turning lines are charged with sensuous responses. There is energy in this voluptuous figure. She is kinetic, alive, not the studio model paid to hold a frozen position while the drawing proceeds. De Kooning early on had ceased drawing from the model, but like many great artists, retained a trove of images in his mind. The lines convey a sense of vital animation in forming their rubicund configurations. Even in black and white there is a colorful sense of life.

Untitled (Woman), c. 1974

Charcoal on vellum mounted on board, 66½ x 42 (168.9 x 106.7)

Purchase, with funds from the Grace Belt Endowed Purchase Fund, the Wilfred P. and Rose J. Cohen Purchase Fund, the Dana Foundation, Incorporated, The List Purchase Fund, the Norman and Rosita Winston Foundation, Inc., and the Drawing Committee   85.23

PROVENANCE

The artist; anonymous owner; Stephen Mazoh and Co., New York

Lucas Samaras

b. 1936

More intensely than most recent draftsmen, Samaras has sought technical invention in the use of materials. Not only has he probably employed the widest variety of technical innovations in drawing, but he has also evolved diverse styles to do so. He invents a style for nearly every series of drawings he makes. These always remain holistic expressions in themselves, and rarely are considered as studies for sculpture or other works. Comparing the two drawings in this exhibition, we realize how difficult it is to describe the developmental changes in the artist's hand in either one.

The words in Samaras' drawings illustrate a direct response to specific situations in his life. "There is truth in symbols," he has stated. Words have appeared in his art as written texts since the late 1950s, and beginning in the early 1960s, became a major motif in his pastel drawings. Thus, he acknowledges the use of words as graphic configurations as well as for their literary associations.

In *Extra Large Drawing No. 2*, Samaras has employed a most distinctive drawing implement, the hypodermic needle, to produce an ejected line that exploits Jackson Pollock's thrown rhythmic line. But Samaras has transformed the older artist's line, condensing it into miniature and thereby increasing its emotional charge. The four-quadrant structure of the composition lends stability to a busy, agitated surface. The letters, from upper left to lower right, spell DRAW. The baroque eyelash-style lines demarcate each letter in black ink on the white paper, so that the letter reads as if it might have been carved in white plaster. The hand of the artist is not given to gracious writing in this drawing, but expresses the act of a compulsive image maker.

Extra Large Drawing No. 2, 1975

Ink on paper, 30¼ x 22 (76.8 x 55.9)

Purchase, with funds from the Crawford Foundation   77.69

PROVENANCE
The artist; The Pace Gallery, New York

EXHIBITIONS
WMAA 1978, p. 55; WMAA 1979, n.p.

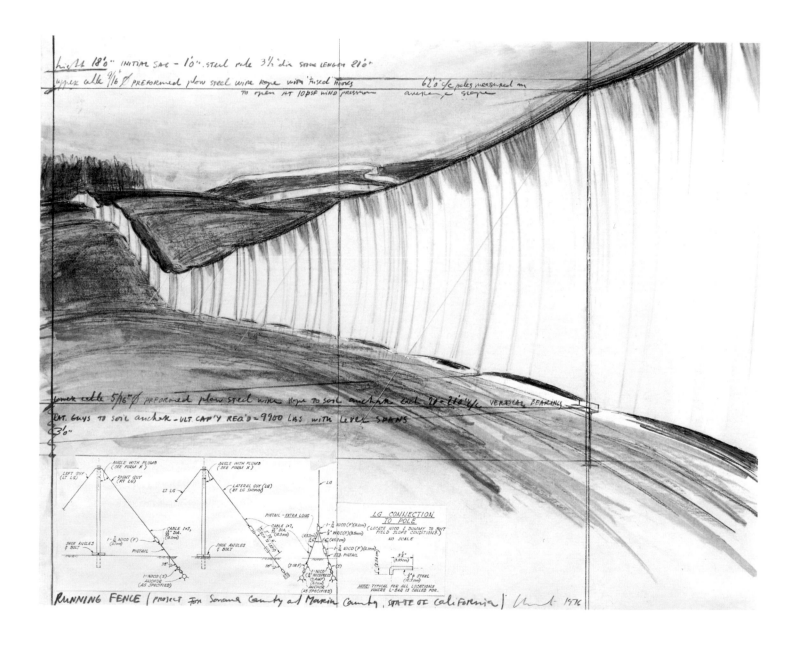

RUNNING FENCE (PROJECT FOR Sonoma County and Marin County, STATE OF California) Christo 1976

Christo

b. 1935

Running Fence, Project for Sonoma County and Marin County, State of California, 1976

Collage, 22 x 28 (55.9 x 71.1)

Purchase, with funds from the Paul Rewald Memorial Fund   77.20

PROVENANCE

The artist; Running Fence Corporation, New York

EXHIBITIONS

WMAA 1978, p. 24; Whitney Museum of American Art, New York, *The Decade in Review: Selections from the 1970s,* 1979, n.p.; Miami University Art Museum, Oxford, Ohio, *A Seventies Selection from the Collection of the Whitney Museum of American Art,* 1981, pp. 11–12; Whitney Museum of American Art, Fairfield County, Stamford, Connecticut, *Surveying the Seventies: Selections from the Permanent Collection of the Whitney Museum of American Art,* 1982, n.p.; WMAA 1983, n.p.

A significant aspect of Christo's art is his engagement with the public in the realization of his projects. By wrapping politically sensitive monuments and cultural institutions or, as he did with the *Running Fence,* by segmenting the property of the citizenry, he designed an art to provoke. The idea of the fence was born in 1972. The following year a site in northern California's Sonoma and Marin counties was located. There followed three years of ecological and engineering feasibility studies, litigation, hearings, public relations, and entertainments on the part of Christo to gain approval. The fence he proposed would not endanger humans, the earth, the sea, or the livestock.

To finance such vast undertakings, Christo makes drawings, of which *Running Fence, Project for Sonoma County and Marin County, State of California* is an example. Not only do these drawings reveal the concept, but they often predocument the results. Using photomontage and collage, incorporating mechanical drawings and other bits of information or materials, Christo unifies the visual data through his own draftsmanship. Embellishing his work with annotations, words, charts, and the drawing marks themselves, he establishes the feeling of participation in the creation of the work. The artist's energy is transmitted to the viewer through the intimacy of his unifying handwriting and drawing marks. The ghostlike quality of his fences, wrapped buildings, or monuments exhibits his sense of the theatrical and continues to haunt the mind.

Christo's drawing methods are direct. He is not concerned with an excessive display of style. A studied practicality reveals itself in the careful shading on the cloth, the perspectival statement of the fence, and the dark russet colors of the distant landscape. The foreground—with its engineering design, the grid measurements that fix the pole heights and angles for the struts and anchoring blocks—engages the eye and mind. Writing and words themselves have an honored place in modern art, especially since the rise of Cubism, Futurism, and Concrete poetry. Christo uses writing to record practical notes and facts, but the words communicate as if they had been sent to each viewer individually. The impact of such drawings is not so different from that of reading a provocative letter addressed to someone else.

Al Held

b. 1928

By the mid-1970s, Al Held had evolved an impressively individualistic approach to geometric painting essentially unrelated to the earlier twentieth-century schools of Constructivism or Neo-plasticism. His Abstract Expressionist paintings of the mid-1950s are marked by richly colored, heavily pigmented surfaces which exhibit compact gestures. These configurations can now be seen as having made a significant contribution to the structure of his recent paintings. From 1967 on, a series of linear black-and-white paintings explored related spatial concepts, an exploration encouraged by the enthusiasm Held developed for Baroque architecture during a trip to Rome. The circle, rectangle, arc, and other basic geometric shapes are set in designs that argue for shifting approaches to the experience of space. Held reached an evocative resolution of these ideas in the drawings and paintings of the mid-1970s such as *76 C–7*.

Held, like Josef Albers and others, employs the straightedge or compass to draw. Unlike the older artist, he uses color in his drawings and for some years has incorporated small shapes from architectural templates to animate his planar configurations. These Baroque-like constructions are drawn with a compound line built of parallel striations. The lines meet at corners that are calculated to suggest which plane should move forward or which recede. This does not necessarily guarantee an illusionistic space in the mind's eye because of the incomplete nature of certain perspectival configurations. What Held establishes in these drawings and paintings is an obsessive metamorphosis. In this multiform reading, structural contradictions are often implied or stated by the templates—circles, ovals, or arcs—which stress the frontality of the picture plane and just as equally destroy it. Transparencies are developed by the template shapes, which together agitate the spatial statement. Each visual reading is quickly eclipsed by a new and novel transformation.

The role of the artist's hand in drawings such as these, which are intellectually evocative, resides less in the development of a refined gesture than in the hand's severe implementations of an image, whether it is preconceived or is developed in an arbitrary fashion. Held stands in direct contrast to Cy Twombly, whose line is charged with emotional content, or to Albers, with his visual witticisms. In these oppositions we find the great richness of modern American drawings.

76 C–7, 1976

Colored pencil, graphite, crayon, and felt-tip pen on paper, 27 x 39¹⁵⁄₁₆ (68.6 x 101.4)

Purchase, with funds from the Drawing Committee   86.2

PROVENANCE

The artist; André Emmerich Gallery, New York; Barbara Toll Fine Arts, New York

Ellsworth Kelly

b. 1923

Nearly a decade and a half after making *Briar*, Kelly was using severe geometric shapes with sophisticated refinement. *Black Triangle with White* served as a study for a painting and relates to a series of low relief wall constructions. In this drawing with collage, Kelly has moved from his initial inspiration in nature to shapes already extant in his paintings or sculptures. These basic geometric forms are now drawn with a straightedge or cut with scissors. The shapes communicate with the viewer because they project the artist's ability, refined with experience, to endow them with visual tensions.

The nearly square format of the sheet contains an image that reinforces the linear rectangle, which dramatically cuts diagonally across the page's center. Since dark tones usually recede, the black triangle could be read as an open vista on this white surface. It also exerts a downward visual weight on the rectangle, establishing a slight optical torque.

Shapes in Kelly drawings are often concerned with static or active positions. This drawing suggests an active reading because the triangle and the wide white bar both pivot on dramatic angles. Although the artist's touch in the line is removed by his mechanical implements, its psychological presence is felt. Drawings of this nature require of the artist the most exquisite sensibility to be effective. Their beauty resides in the tension of threat and, finally, in their stability, since the threat is never executed.

Black Triangle with White, 1977

Collage and ink on paper, 31½ x 34½
(80 x 87.6)

Purchase, with funds from Philip Morris
Incorporated   78.100

PROVENANCE

The artist; Leo Castelli Gallery, New York

EXHIBITIONS

WMAA 1979, n.p.; Whitney Museum of
American Art, New York, *The Decade in
Review: Selections from the 1970s*, 1979,
n.p.; WMAA 1981, p. 29; WMAA 1981a,
n.p.; WMAA 1982, n.p.

Roy Lichtenstein

b. 1923

Roy Lichtenstein in recent years has turned to the examination of his early Pop subject matter in a tightly composed drawing-collage mode. His use of collage, either with cut paper or as a method of assembling images, is revealed in its fullness in Study for *Figures in Landscape*. This composition discloses his interest in Léger, Picasso, and other modern masters, whose characteristic styles or forms are wedded to many of Lichtenstein's own famous images. The doe-eyed girl in profile, the mirror, the architectural fragment, the sailboat, the plant à la Picasso, the eye-mouth motif, the sea and landscape, and the cloud-filled sky are all images Lichtenstein once considered individually rather than in juxtaposition, as in this disturbing biomorphic synthesis.

The running thick lines which emerged in Lichtenstein's Ben-Day dot drawings and paintings is retained here and functions as a graphic device that unifies the composition, as do the rigid stripes that represent shadows. His method of drawing a line and reinforcing it so that it echoes the thick lines seen in cartoons results in a curious portrait of a line and disguises the artist's hand.

Study for *Figures in Landscape* is a still-life image which is neither a *vanitas* nor a celebration of nature's fecundity. Rather it is a collection of man-made objects, save for the figurative references, which suggests in its highly refined style that these broken, disjointed bits are shards of a world not right with itself. The image proclaims that the technique of collage is, in recent art, as forceful as the structural concepts of Cubism or the emotional importunings of Surrealism, which are also evident. The highly mannered style of current art trends is expressed in a form of Baroque mannerism with swirling curvilinear elements. No longer do we find the friendly images of Pop art, with their warm supermarket reality or TV charm, but a disturbing world where the images proclaim a fallen culture.

Study for **Figures in Landscape**, 1977

Graphite and colored pencil with collage on paper, 22½ x 27¾ (57.2 x 70.5)

Purchase, with funds from the Drawing Committee   84.4

PROVENANCE

The artist; James Goodman Gallery, New York

EXHIBITIONS

James Goodman Gallery, New York, *Roy Lichtenstein: A Drawing Retrospective*, 1984, p. 43; WMAA 1985, p. 34

Chuck Close

b. 1940

Phil/Fingerprint II, 1978
Stamp-pad ink and graphite on paper,
29¾ x 22¼ (75.6 x 56.5)
Purchase, with funds from Peggy and
Richard Danziger   78.55

PROVENANCE

The artist; The Pace Gallery, New York

EXHIBITIONS

WMAA 1978, p. 25; The Pace Gallery,
New York, *Chuck Close*, 1979; Danforth
Museum, Framingham, Massachusetts,
Directions in Realism, 1980; Walker Art
Center, Minneapolis, *Close Portraits*, 1980,
p. 22 (traveled); Pennsylvania Academy of
the Fine Arts, Philadelphia, *Contemporary
American Realism Since 1960*, 1981, p. 10;
Whitney Museum of American Art, New
York, organizer, *American Art Since 1970:
Painting, Sculpture, and Drawings from the
Collection of the Whitney Museum of
American Art*, 1984, pp. 40–41 (traveled);
WMAA 1986, n. p.

The grid system is an ancient device for transferring an image from a small drawing onto a larger canvas or a wall. A rigid geometric construct, the grid holds the image onto the page, thereby affecting our perception. Chuck Close's grids are part of his multiple mark-making systems. His early spray paintings were followed by hatching systems, fingerprints, and other devices that reveal a graphic sensibility. He makes photographs of friends, which then can serve either for drawings or paintings. In *Phil/Fingerprint II*, he begins by working on the top line in the left corner, proceeds across the page, then moves one line down, and onward until he reaches the bottom. Each mark reconstructs tones equivalent to those occupying the corresponding square on the small grid. This working method echoes similar systems employed by the Minimalist artists. The construction of an image according to a preconceived ritual method suggests greater concern with the process and concept of making than with the plumbing of the subject's psychological depths. Close's *Phil*, therefore, is not traditional portraiture.

The subject of *Phil* is really the artist as creator—his rules, his observation of the world, his insight into systems of thinking, process, or of architectonic reconstruction. That Close has inventively used the airbrush, fingerprints, or a variety of hatchings argues a need for new devices that explore the range and quality of the artist's statements, rather than the subject's personality. Each shift in graphic means therefore becomes a comment on the role of style in the artist's oeuvre. Close demonstrates that even such shifting technical processes retain the artist's touch.

Another conceivable reading of this drawing is as a monotype, a single printed image turned on the tip of the artist's finger instead of issuing from traditional metal or glass surfaces. These monumental Ben-Day dots stress the surface of the page because they are on the picture plane as well as on the physical surface of the paper. From a certain distance, the mind blends the dots into a quasi-three-dimensional image that remotely recalls the work's photographic origins.

Bill Jensen

b. 1945

The drawings of Bill Jensen, either linear constructions such as *Black Line Drawing* or dusky charcoal modulations which coalesce into biomorphic forms, are generally studies for paintings. They also occur during the painting process as aids to the resolution of pictorial problems. A sketchbook is used to record ideas that are expanded into presentation drawings or paintings. *Black Line Drawing*, however, is a re-examination of a motif that appears in the 1976–77 painting *Redon*.

Jensen's imagery suggests sources in nature—an effect that belies his working process. He begins by making a series of arcs, lines, or arbitrary marks on the page. Once an image is established, he makes further additions, relying on the interplay of his imagination with the established shapes as they build into new forms. Most of his images are individualistic and interrelate only with each other within the broad terms of a large visual vocabulary. In *Black Line Drawing*, Jensen achieves two eccentric mandorla configurations which move like a whirlpool galaxy. Occasionally he will draw on both sides of the vellum, thereby increasing the range of tones and producing a shadowy opaque image which stands behind and sometimes echoes or acts dissonantly with the main image.

Building a compound line made with thick sticks of graphite whose dense black is plied layer upon layer in repeated gestures, Jensen creates a heavy ragged-edged line. The image suggests natural forms such as buds or petals, plantlike figurations of fecundity. His images do not flaunt their content, but demand tranquil contemplation to divulge their message.

Black Line Drawing, 1978

Graphite and charcoal on vellum, 24 x 19 (61 x 48.3)

Purchase, with funds from the Mr. and Mrs. M. Anthony Fisher Purchase Fund 82.19

PROVENANCE

The artist; Washburn Gallery, New York

EXHIBITIONS

WMAA 1985, p. 29

"Death lies on her, like an
untimely frost —
Upon the sweetest flower of
the field."
Shakespeare

H. C. Westermann

b. 1922

The mythologies of a sailor's life inform the art of H. C. Westermann. His literary tastes, which range from Shakespeare to comics and tabloids, are augmented by fantasies inspired by the movies. Who are the characters animating his usually dark views of the sea, the desert, or landscapes? In *The Sweetest Flower,* a late work, we see a self-portrait transformed into the guise of Clark Gable: Westermann loved cigars and, having been an acrobat in the circus, remained in fine physical trim. What manner of bird, fixed with its searchlight eye, like the weighty albatross, illuminates the object of this sailor's waterfront desire? The ominous dark tramp freighter that appears throughout his art is always a symbol of foreboding. Here it moves beneath a lowering sky, whose slender crescent moon reflects little light from behind black clouds.

Westermann draws his mythic world in a style endowed with the most common of sources, yet with profound seriousness. It is this intent which enhances our response and engenders our willingness to accept his formulations. Westermann's work differs from the output of a cartoonist in that he has experienced the content examined in his art, rendering it poignant, in contrast to the illustrator's artificiality. What initially appears as crude is a carefully evolved style.

The Sweetest Flower, 1978

Watercolor on "Green" paper, 22⅛ x 31 (56.2 x 78.7)

Purchase, with funds from The Lauder Foundation—Drawing Fund   78.102

PROVENANCE

The artist; Xavier Fourcade Gallery, New York

EXHIBITIONS

WMAA 1979, n.p.; WMAA 1981, p. 64; WMAA 1981a, n.p.; Xavier Fourcade Gallery, New York, *H. C. Westermann,* 1981

NOTHING CONFORMS TO X SPECK STATIONS .. FANCY REAM ARGÙS AND A LIL FALTER PEACE WHILE WAITING FOR THE MODEL ..
SHADOWSLICKASEALSLITHERTHROUGH

William T. Wiley

b. 1937

The drawings and watercolors of William T. Wiley are anecdotal, permeated with a rustic Western atmosphere and a novel iconography. Filled with layered, camouflaged images, they demand time from the viewer who wants to recognize and appreciate the interconnecting design. The bold areas are readily perceived, but the subtle spirit which inhabits these works commands study. In this watercolor, Wiley not only tricks the eye, but he also includes subchapters and minor characters as if in a story. *Nothing Conforms* is a view of the artist's studio. On the distant wall is a painting in progress, yet on reconsideration it becomes a mirror reflecting what is behind the location where the viewer stands.

Many strange objects inhabit the studio. There are the artist's tools: palettes, easel, brushes, and props, but what role does the sign for infinity have in this scheme of things? The rough edges that seem like carved logs are decorated with incursions that read as the head of a moose or bird, while elephant heads project from the two slippers and stalactites or icicles hang down from the top edge. Objects float, or are discernible on one plane at one minute and shift at the next viewing—"Nothing," the caption begins, "conforms to X Speck Stations." Imaginative space here has few references to the real world of experience.

Wiley has conceived a large vocabulary of images and motifs with which to tell his tales, and this drawing is one of his most complete anthologies. His sources in comic humor, bucolic life, and the studio or outdoors combine to form puzzles that become rewarding to solve. His masterful watercolor technique, which allows him to layer many colors, keeping each in sophisticated separate images, is unmatched today. In his form of still-life interior, the viewer's endless speculations are goaded by the text as well as by the images themselves.

Nothing Conforms, 1978

Watercolor on paper, 29½ x 22½
(74.9 x 57.2)

Purchase, with funds from the Neysa McMein Purchase Award   79.25

PROVENANCE

The artist; Allan Frumkin Gallery, New York

EXHIBITIONS

Whitney Museum of American Art, New York, *The Decade in Review: Selections from the 1970s*, 1979, n.p.; Walker Art Center, Minneapolis, *Wiley Territory*, 1980, p. 46; WMAA 1983, n.p.; The Hudson River Museum, Yonkers, New York, *Form or Formula: Drawing and Drawings*, 1986, p. 52

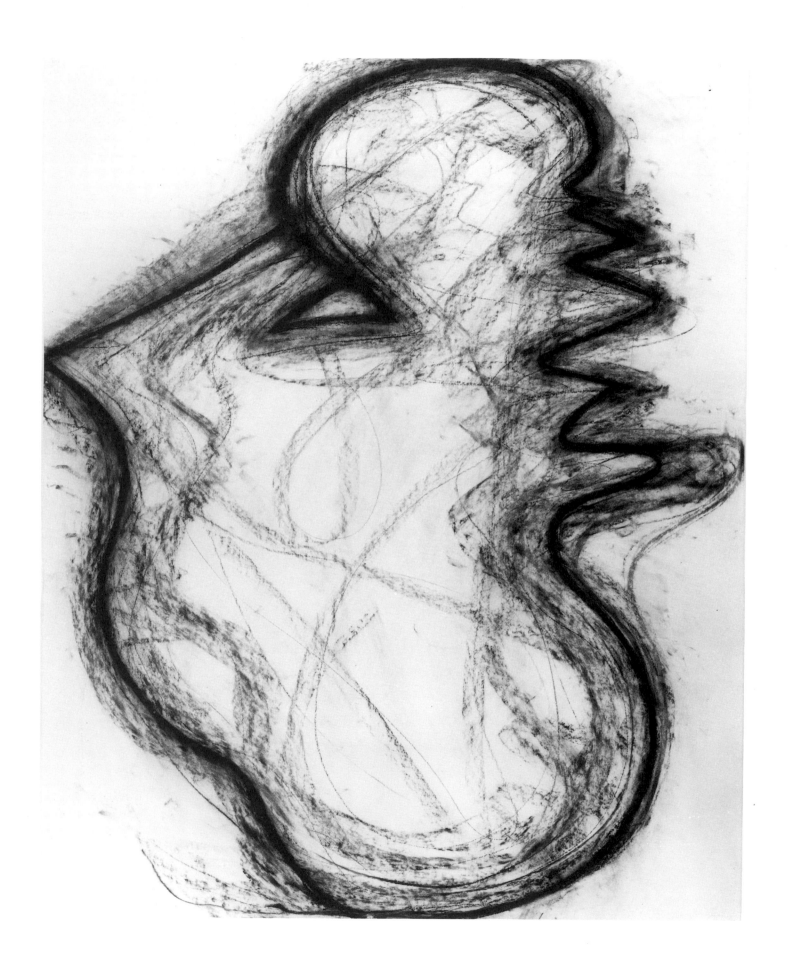

Elizabeth Murray

b. 1940

One of the great attractions of abstract art is its power of mutable suggestion. Its ambiguities permit, if not demand, ever new responses as the viewer garners increased knowledge through experience. Its character is finally defined, when, and if, new interpretations cease. In this light we can enjoy the post-biomorphic drawings of Elizabeth Murray.

She usually begins working with some object in mind, a still life or a figure, but in *Shake* the object is less apparent than the process of making the drawing. Thin running lines ricochet across the surface from point to point, setting out a rough configuration enhanced by the thick end of a stick of charcoal. A wide black compound line is employed to refine the shape's identity in the complete composition.

The subject appears to be derived less from the physical objects that appear in most of Murray's work than from a construction of symbolic stimulae for sensations. The bulbous, polymorphic fecund shapes, described in an elastic line, could be interpreted as a torso. And the variety of lines and breathing, tensil quality suggest pregnancy and birth with their physical and psychological changes. But to stress anthropomorphization is to reduce our experience of the drawing by directing it toward a figural resolution, rather than toward high abstraction. Murray's images evolve away from the initiating motif and if we attempt to return to it we narrow the breadth of our experience.

Shake, 1979

Charcoal on paper, 46½ x 38
(118.1 x 96.5)

Purchase, with funds from Joel and Anne
Ehrenkranz   79.60

PROVENANCE

The artist; Paula Cooper Gallery,
New York

EXHIBITIONS

WMAA 1981, p. 35; WMAA 1981a, n.p.;
WMAA 1982, n.p.

Jonathan Borofsky

b. 1942

Self-Portrait at 2668379 and 2670098,
1979–80

Acrylic and charcoal on paper,
84¾ x 48 (215.3 x 121.9)

Purchase, with funds from Joel and
Anne Ehrenkranz   82.3

PROVENANCE

The artist; Paula Cooper Gallery,
New York

EXHIBITIONS

Whitney Museum of American Art, Fairfield
County, Stamford, Connecticut, *Entering
the Eighties*, 1983; n.p.; Whitney Museum
of American Art, New York, organizer,
*American Art Since 1970: Painting, Sculp-
ture, and Drawings from the Collection of
the Whitney Museum of American Art*,
1984, pp. 34–35 (traveled); WMAA
1985, p. 19

For centuries the self-portrait has served the artist as subject matter for
momentary or studied documentation, for metamorphic or meditative
examinations. A contemporary exponent of the self-portrait is Jonathan
Borofsky. His images arise in his dreams, to be recorded in drawings on
small, even tiny scraps of paper. Not depictions of himself, but his entire
dream life constitute much of the imagery and content of his art.

Borofsky's dialogue with his dream life emerged after some years spent
making art associated with the Minimal and Conceptual schools. In 1969
he began counting, from one to infinity, placing lines of numbers across
sheets of paper. This ritualistic activity soon became a post-Minimal,
Conceptual, and therapeutic process. As a linear travelogue through his
psychic life, the numbers established a sequence along which it is theo-
retically possible to locate each of his major expressions. *Self-Portrait at
2668379 and 2670098* began as a dream image recorded as a tiny pencil
sketch. Borofsky then used an opaque projector to enlarge the sketch into
wall drawings, independent drawings on paper such as this one, or into
paintings. This same image was later reconsidered in an enlarged, semi-
rigid painting now in The Museum of Modern Art, New York.

The great standing image endowed with extended horns represents animal
nature, although the gender of the torso is ambiguous. Upon its forehead
is inscribed a triangle crossed with a heart, which forms the star of David,
an important symbol of self-identity for Borofsky. The figure holds a
fragment of a circle or an arc or even a rope such as those used by gym-
nasts or circus performers. Its stance is one of incipient motion.

Behind this standing figure is a large, open-mouthed head in left profile.
In an earlier version, the head was drawn as a mass of fish, while here it
has reached greater human specificity. It establishes a turbulent, colorful
surface behind the stark, carefully drawn frontal figure. The head seems to
be painted on a backdrop which falls to the floor. To date, this is the quin-
tessential self-portrait of the artist as performer. Does it also suggest that
behind a reserved public façade screams a figure in terror? Is the artist
a risk-taking entertainer?

Richard Diebenkorn

b. 1922

In late 1955, Richard Diebenkorn ceased to be an abstract painter, turning to a figurative vocabulary stated in painterly, flattened, interlocking robust forms. This aesthetic developed partly as a result of his visit to a Matisse exhibition in Los Angeles in the summer of 1952. The next significant turning point was in 1967, when he moved from San Francisco to Santa Monica, where he returned to abstract painting. It was his intention "to achieve a balance with the pictorial elements of light, space, form, line, and composition simultaneously." In order to accomplish this and not succumb to a mannered system, he began what he refers to as "a dialogue with the work."

His method, evident in *Untitled*, a drawing that broadly relates to his Ocean Park series of paintings, is to begin by placing arbitrary marks on the working surface. This establishes an inchoate basis for the composition. For the artist it means "going into an unknown situation." Working without a preconceived configuration, Diebenkorn sought to move these abstract elements to achieve compositions that would "look as though they were *meant* to be there."

What has emerged from this activity are large areas of luminous color held in place either by geometric markings, as in this drawing, or by free-hand curviform shapes in others. The working and reworkings, evident in the pentimenti, are brushed down to reduce their presence, but nevertheless remain as ghostlike striations in the composition. Purity and elegance enrich these designs. While the Ocean Park series has lost many of its referential sources in the metropolitan landscape or the architectural geometry of interiors, works such as *Untitled* remain vitalized by these sources.

The best of Diebenkorn's work maintains the frontality of Abstract Expressionist pictures, a unification of the picture plane and the image. His images are less on the surface than *of* the surface. They are the results of the artist's formal concerns, examined through a serendipitous imagination, blended in a seductive California light.

Untitled, 1980

Oil on paper, 38 x 25 (96.5 x 63.5)

Purchase, with funds from Joel and Anne Ehrenkranz   80.41

PROVENANCE

The artist; M. Knoedler and Co., New York

EXHIBITIONS

WMAA 1981, p. 17; WMAA 1981a, n.p.; WMAA 1982, n.p.

Philip Guston

1913–1980

One always sensed that Guston was never completely at ease with total abstraction. The break with abstraction came in 1967–68, when with great energy he burst upon the art scene with new figurative images painted in the same richly modulated, colored lines that he had employed in the abstractions. These new figures were fragments of bodies, shoes, books, bottles, clocks, and a vast assortment of domestic still-life objects. Also returning were the early hooded figures seen in the drawing for *Conspirators,* but now they were given cigars, vertical slits for eyes, and often seemed engaged in some non-serious mayhem. In many ways, they have assumed the role of the artist—working on easel paintings, lurking in automobiles, buried in fields covered with the merchandise of mass marketing.

Untitled, an ink drawing made in the last few months of Guston's life, is a summation of his observations on life and art. A field of strange domestic objects, body parts, clouds, misbegotten rubber tires, rugs, hammers, and escapees from man's midden are rushing forward to the tops of two buried heads at the lower part of the sheet. On the left is a portrait of the artist in profile with a single glaring eye and, on the right, his wife, her hair barely visible. A curious portent is the artist's signature on a rock, all too suggestive of a headstone. Is this Guston's vision of the future? A debased junk-covered landscape awaiting man's last potlatch? His resilient humor is stated in bulky forms which in their crudity enhance the poignancy of his observations. The line continues with the same flowing ease of the abstract drawings. These lumpy cartoonish configurations immediately exerted a great influence on a younger generation of artists.

Is it a strange turn of events that an artist whose paintings in his youth were filled with social satire and humor should return to them later in life? After a certain age, the memory retains youthful images with a clarity not found in its recording of recent events. Guston was famous for his succinct and often biting cartoons of art world celebrities. Has he not, in his late work, turned his pen on himself with equal vigor and insight?

Untitled, 1980

Ink on paper, 20 x 30 (50.8 x 76.2)

Purchase, with funds from Mr. and Mrs. William A. Marsteller and Agneta Gruss 81.6

PROVENANCE

Estate of the artist; David McKee Gallery, New York

EXHIBITIONS

The Phillips Collection, Washington, D.C., *Philip Guston, 1980: The Last Works,* 1981, p. 31 (traveled); WMAA 1981, p. 27

Jim Nutt

b. 1938

A cofounder of the Hairy Who, a group of six Chicago artists who began showing collectively in 1966, Nutt reflected their general interest in mannered drawing, intense coloration, sexually charged imagery, and motifs which were transformed from suburban life, the media, and other forms of common culture. Like many of the group, he had studied at the relatively traditional School of the Art Institute. Abstraction, never a strong influence in Chicago, had little or no appeal to Nutt and his generation. They were concerned with using the world about them to engage their aesthetic fantasies. Their form of realism is intense: the seedy world of the city's back streets provides several of the Hairy Who with their visual vocabularies.

The stage, or a containerlike room, is frequently the setting for the drama of Nutt's images. He employs several types of figures, of which three appear in *Hi—I'm so Happy:* tiny figures who always seem to be vying for the attention of larger figures, and ghostly balloonlike heads that upstage these central figures. The theatrical surrealism Nutt invokes sometimes conceals his sources in comic books, graffiti, folk art, and other less-than-high art. Removed from traditional modes of representation, the figure as used by Nutt is often explicit, yet non-erotic.

Nutt's drawing skills are refined and inventive as he orchestrates the different characters in their enigmatic tale. The exaggerated musculature of the body builder or the diminutive figures of the fools, servants, or entertainers are stated in a carefully executed technique which could easily have been derived from Seurat, tinctured with the colors found in neon lights. The interaction between the demanding male and the resisting female with a mirror in her hand suggests a version of the *vanitas* theme, therefore a literary association, which often informs much of Chicago art. Nutt's art can be read as a series of chapters in an ongoing drama. Yet, inevitably, it is the quality of the drawing which is exciting—its tightly controlled lines and forms with no superfluous graphic flourishes.

Hi—I'm So Happy (If a Bit Silly), 1981

Colored pencil on paper, 10⅞ x 16
(27.6 x 40.6)

Purchase, with funds from Philip Morris
Incorporated   81.15

PROVENANCE

The artist; Phyllis Kind Gallery, New York

EXHIBITIONS

WMAA 1981, p. 37; WMAA 1981a, n.p.

Richard Hunt

b. 1935

Sculptors' drawings frequently suggest the rigid schematic façade of architectural renderings enlivened by the play of the hand in moments of invention. Often they are portraits of completed sculptures; other times, they are multifold examinations of forms before work commences in three dimensions. But the best are those which demonstrate inventive imagery and display a bold handwriting. Richard Hunt's drawings, along with those of David Smith, Theodore Roszak, and Lucas Samaras, are among the most exciting produced in the latter half of the twentieth century.

In 1953, Hunt saw the sculpture of Julio Gonzalez and undertook the challenge of welded metal. His early work was assembled from pieces of junk, welded together much like the constructions of Richard Stankiewicz, Joseph Goto, and others in the 1950s. Living in Chicago, which has long supported a Surrealist-informed invention, Hunt used industrial refuse, blending in rods, pipes, and other manufactured elements. His major expression is stated in a linear form which is as viable in his sculpture as in his drawings.

In recent years, Hunt has developed a brightly colored palette in his drawings. Oil pastels radiate an inner luminosity, charging their colors with high-key brightness. Here the bonelike shapes and the biomorphic structures glow against the white surface of the paper. Menacing, predatory, vegetative, these shapes reach across the horizon as if they were the final grasping gesture of some now lost prehistoric monster. The shapes seem destined to be sculpture. Most of Hunt's drawings, however, are conceptual and not always destined for specific sculptures. The elements in this drawing seem to be less musings on a single theme than shapes erupting in one place and continuing elsewhere, which suggests that they represent sections of a much larger object.

Untitled, 1982

Oil pastel on paper, 23 x 29 (58.4 x 73.7)

Purchase, with funds from Richard Brown Baker and Mr. and Mrs. William A. Marsteller   83.21

PROVENANCE

The artist; Terry Dintenfass Gallery, New York

EXHIBITIONS

WMAA 1983, n.p.; WMAA 1985, p. 29

Fahrenheit 1982°   colored inks   James Rosenquist 1982

James Rosenquist

b. 1933

Color set in a bold graphic image generates a vitality in Rosenquist's drawings, which is augmented by their grand scale. For some years, he has utilized a tripartite composition that jams three seemingly disparate images into near equal sections of the horizontal format. Within each part can be read a specific still-life image selected from the miasmic worlds of print and advertising. While the image used may change, Rosenquist continues to employ a series of abstract forms that find their manifestation in these transmuted icons. The lipsticks—suggestive, erotic, thrusing—point their way from an anonymous background; the molten metal pouring from a cauldron like melted butter evokes a horrifying contrast to the face of the smiling young girl under the hairdryer in *F-111*, the famous painting of 1965. The pen-tipped finger is a symbolic portrait of the writer Judith Goldman, who prefers to write at night, as the earth spins under an umbrella of star tracks. Visually these different elements suggest a rebus which, on examination, remains a mystery.

Many of the best American drawings of this century are painterly, that is, they use oil paint, inks, watercolors, and synthetic media, applied with brushes. Rosenquist's sheets differ from his paintings in that they are physically smaller and explore new imagery and techniques, thereby transmitting an energy not always experienced in the more carefully planned paintings. The elegant manipulation of the brush and inks produces the luminous, seductive nature of *Fahrenheit 1982°*. The inks' brilliant hues serve as a foil for the cloudy, indefinite atmosphere of the mylar. The traditional linear drawing methods are subsumed in Rosenquist's ability to set areas of tone as if they were spray-painted. Mottled surfaces, the variety of lines, and the intense bright light are always carefully controlled.

Fahrenheit 1982°, 1982

Colored ink on frosted mylar, 33⅛ x 71½ (84.1 x 181.6)

...ith funds from the John I. H.
...nase Fund, the Mr. and Mrs. M.
...isher Purchase Fund, and The
...oundation—Drawing Fund   82.35

PROVENANCE

The artist; Castelli-Feigen-Corcoran, New York

EXHIBITIONS

Museum of Fine Arts, Boston, *10 Painters and Sculptors Draw*, 1984, no. 9; WMAA 1985, p. 48

STONES
are
our
Food

03 mai 82-84

Cy Twombly

b. 1929

During the years 1982 to 1984, Cy Twombly produced a series of five drawings, all of large format, which represented his response to an article in *National Geographic* about certain stones which absorbed water during the rainy season and discharged it during times of drought, thereby keeping the land moist. They aided the production of food, and this formed a poetic image in the artist's mind. It seems that such stones are found in Armenia, which was the homeland of Arshile Gorky. And so the series of drawings is dedicated to the older artist.

The development of Twombly's drawings constitutes a slow shift from sheets filled with multiple shapes in various interrelationships to the recent works, where the format is larger and the individual images bigger and fewer in number. In *Untitled,* the words across the top offer a message: "Stones Are Our Food to Gorky." Written just below are the dates of the drawing and, still lower, a series of configurations drawn one over the other to suggest urns or a toy ship. Each image is drawn in different colors, with contrasting materials and individual line styles. What initially seems like a tension-filled series of graffiti markings reads, upon consideration, as abstracted shapes, similar to those which have appeared in Twombly's art for decades. If one of these shapes is an urn, does the series of flowing lines depict the water flowing outward to nurture the earth? Twombly only hints, indicates, feints, and always in a poetic mode. The substance of his drawings—even when there are written references to classical literature—remains a series of highly charged abstract tracks. These nervous, brittle, angular, wiry lines, each with its own message, bear more content individually than collectively. Twombly's drawings are among the most difficult late twentieth-century works to apprehend and appreciate.

Untitled (Stones Are Our Food to Gorky), 1982–84

Oil pastel, crayon, and graphite on paper, 44½ x 30⅛ (113 x 76.5)

Gift of the artist   84.30

PROVENANCE

The artist

EXHIBITIONS

CDS Gallery, New York, *Artists Choose Artists,* 1984; WMAA 1985, p. 61

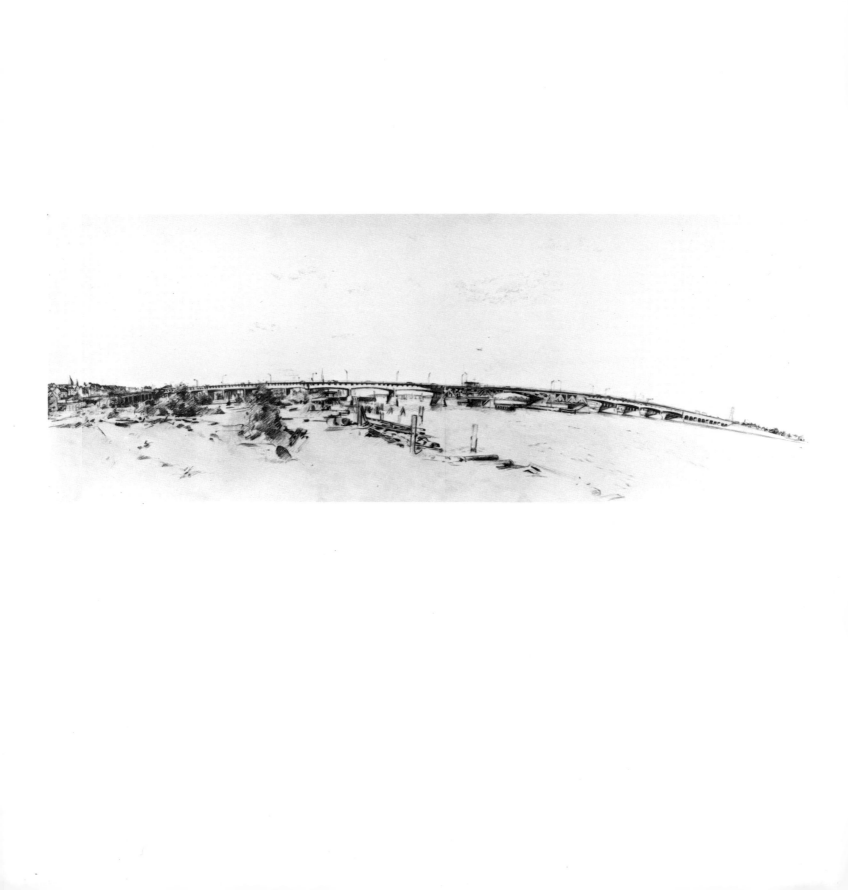

Rackstraw Downes

b. 1939

Realism, like so many other schools of art, suffers from the polemics of definition. Is realism a transcription of nature or a socio-political response to man's struggle? Does Downes' *Million Dollar Bridge* reveal man's inventive nature in conceiving this brilliant engineering feat to span a vast range of water, or is this bridge an economic device to provide work and thereby sustain local business?

Another position might be that the spanning arc against sky and water had a visual appeal to the artist. The drawings of Rackstraw Downes usually serve as studies for paintings, as did this one. His bridge echoes Whistler's etched views of Venice, though the older artist set the city at a distance over a broad expanse of water and illuminated it by the shifting, reflected light from lagoons and waterways. The composition of the Downes' drawing expands toward the lower center while several objects lead our eye to the focus of the action in the left half. The harsh summer light increases our awareness of the structure of this bridge. As it sweeps across the page, the broad perspectival view makes us turn our heads in order to encompass the entire image.

The bold, secure use of graphite articulates this page-spanning vista. Below a bare sky, the bridge itself is drawn with busy shadows and perspectival shiftings. A panorama which begins in light grays in the far distance at right comes forward, only to recede abruptly into a new distance. The physical requirements demanded to view the drawing echo those which are needed to see the actual bridge.

Downes manipulates his tones, stating the most distant elements in light gray, increasing to darker values toward the center, and sustaining these darks as they veer off to the left where shrubs and nautical gear engage the eye. This form of realism aims at a transcription of nature, though reality may not be the picture's subject. The subject could reside in the abstract problem of containing such a lengthy motif clearly within the picture frame, or it could stress the nature of the arc which divides the open sky and the cluttered foreground. Downes' realism describes the day, the qualities of the sunlight, the heat, indeed all the elements which are experienced in such a place at a specific time of the year.

Portland, Me., The Million Dollar Bridge, 1983

Graphite on paper, 19 x 50⅜ (48.3 x 128)

Purchase, with funds from the Drawing Committee   83.42

PROVENANCE

The artist; Hirschl & Adler Modern, New York

EXHIBITIONS

Hirschl & Adler Modern, New York, *Rackstraw Downes*, 1984, p. 19; WMAA 1985, p. 24

Jasper Johns

b. 1930

Jasper Johns entered the art scene at a time when abstraction was the significant fashion of expression. His still-life imagery was therefore shocking, but it also appealed to a literary sensibility that found abstraction difficult. His early imagery evolved into designs fraught with an arcane content.

Johns' drawings serve as studies for paintings, though they are also often drawn after paintings, or produced with the thought of prints in mind. The interweavings between these modes of expression, after three decades of development, are extraordinarily complex. *Untitled*, a charcoal drawing, represents a later meditation on the 1963 painting *Land's End*, which in turn echoes earlier work—the rulers and fan-shaped hemispheres appeared in *Good Time Charley* (1961) and *Device* (1961–62), the misnamed color signs in *Out the Window* (1959). These early pictures were painted in bright colors with short, choppy brushstrokes which animated their surfaces, acknowledging the influence of Abstract Expressionist methods applied to a novel subject matter. Naturally gifted, with a delicate, sensitive touch, Johns has always been attracted to the ancient art of controlling black in his subtle variations of charcoal, ink, and graphite. In this drawing, the surface is gritty, with lines carefully, though easily, drawn, with bold striations to embellish the surface.

The splayed lines issuing from the hand attached to a narrow, charcoal-marked pole refer to the broom Johns attached to a canvas in an earlier work. The word yellow, which had appeared by itself in paintings of the early 1960s, has been enriched by a falling echo, while the word blue, also once in a single panel, now decorates a swag of cloth illusionistically nailed to the lower center. These anthologies of images reconsidered, often years later, reflect the artist's life in the studio, surrounded by the labors of his imagination. They are modern history paintings in which time and image coalesce.

Untitled, 1984

Charcoal on paper, 44 x 33³⁄₁₆
(111.8 x 84.3)

Purchase, with funds from the Burroughs Wellcome Purchase Fund, the Equitable Life Assurance Society of the United States Purchase Fund, the Mr. and Mrs. Thomas M. Evans Purchase Fund and the Mrs. Percy Uris Purchase Fund   86.4

PROVENANCE

The artist

Mel Bochner

b. 1940

In the 1960s, Mel Bochner entered the arena of Conceptualist and Minimalist art. Concept art was essentially a mental, non-visual experience or speculative activity. Bochner, in his early works, employed counting rituals and proportional sequences stated in carefully drawn shapes, to which he then added color. As a student of philosophy and writer of art criticism, he is given to careful explication of many of his working theories and methods.

In the 1980s, Bochner radically changed the outward presentation of his work while retaining its structural foundation. He used oil paint to create a linear, crystalline form-building system. He began drawings on a single sheet of paper, employing a straightedge to lay down the painted lines. As the image developed, he attached additional sheets of paper to accommodate the growth of the composition. These linear constructions, such as *December,* introduce the new elements of light and space to his work. As the lines shift in color, their perspectival relationship with other lines changes; and the irregular triangles they create do not seem to form planes, but an open spatial configuration.

What might mistakenly be read as a mathematically informed configuration in *December* is in reality the felt response to the process of making the drawing, a process that remains visible and animates the image as in many works of the Abstract Expressionists. The polygons which result from these accumulated gestures engage the mind in their spatial interplays.

December, 1984

Oil and enamel on paper, 52⅞ x 45¼
(134.3 x 114.9)

Purchase, with funds from the Drawing
Committee   85.3

PROVENANCE

The artist; Sonnabend Gallery, New York

EXHIBITIONS

Carnegie-Mellon University Art Gallery,
Pittsburgh, *Mel Bochner: 1973–1985,* p. 63;
WMAA 1985, p. 19

Selected Bibliography

Milton Avery

Johnson, Una E., with commemorative essay by Mark Rothko.
Milton Avery: Prints and Drawings 1930–1964.
New York: The Brooklyn Museum, 1966.

Kramer, Hilton. *Milton Avery: Paintings 1930–1960.*
New York: Thomas Yoseloff, 1962.

Milwaukee, David Barnett Gallery. *Milton Avery: A Retrospective of Forty-eight Oils, Watercolors, Gouaches, Drawings, Monotypes, and Original Prints* (exhibition catalogue), 1984. Introduction by David J. Barnett, foreword by Sally Avery, text by Gerald Nordland.

New York, Whitney Museum of American Art. *Milton Avery* (exhibition catalogue), 1982. Catalogue by Barbara Haskell.

Washington, D.C., National Collection of Fine Arts, Smithsonian Institution. *Milton Avery* (exhibition catalogue), 1969. Introduction by Adelyn D. Breeskin.

William Baziotes

Newport Beach, California, Newport Harbor Art Museum. *William Baziotes: A Retrospective Exhibition* (exhibition catalogue), 1978. Introduction by Michael Preble, texts by Barbara Cavaliere and Mona Hadler.

New York, The Solomon R. Guggenheim Museum. *William Baziotes: A Memorial Exhibition* (exhibition catalogue), 1965. Catalogue by Lawrence Alloway.

Thomas Hart Benton

Benton, Thomas Hart. *An American in Art: A Professional and Technical Autobiography.* Lawrence, Kansas: University Press of Kansas, 1969.

————. *Benton Drawings.* Columbia, Missouri: University of Missouri Press, 1968.

Lawrence, Kansas, The University of Kansas Museum of Art. *Thomas Hart Benton* (exhibition catalogue), 1958. Chronology by Thomas Hart Benton.

Marling, Karal Ann. *Tom Benton and His Drawings: A Biographical Essay and a Collection of His Sketches, Studies, and Mural Cartoons.* Columbia, Missouri: University of Missouri Press, 1985.

New Brunswick, New Jersey, Rutgers University Art Gallery. *Thomas Hart Benton: A Retrospective of His Early Years, 1907–1929* (exhibition catalogue), 1972. Catalogue by Phillip Dennis Cate.

Charles Biederman

Biederman, Charles. *Art as the Evolution of Visual Language.* Red Wing, Minnesota: Privately published, 1948.

London, Hayward Gallery, organized by the Arts Council of Great Britain. *Charles Biederman: A Retrospective Exhibition with Special Emphasis on the Structuralist Works of 1936–1969* (exhibition catalogue), 1969. Texts by Robyn Denny and Jan van der Marck.

The Minneapolis Institute of Arts. *Charles Biederman: A Retrospective* (exhibition catalogue), 1976. Introduction by Gregory Hedberg, text by Leif Sjöberg.

Minneapolis, Walker Art Center. *Charles Biederman: The Structuralist Relief 1935–1964* (exhibition catalogue), 1965. Catalogue by Jan van der Marck.

Mel Bochner

The Baltimore Museum of Art. *Mel Bochner: Number and Shape* (exhibition catalogue), 1976. Catalogue by Brenda Richardson.

Pittsburgh, Carnegie-Mellon University Art Gallery. *Mel Bochner: 1973–1985* (exhibition catalogue), 1985. Catalogue by Elaine A. King.

Jonathan Borofsky

Philadelphia Museum of Art in association with the Whitney Museum of American Art, New York. *Jonathan Borofsky* (exhibition catalogue), 1984. Catalogue by Mark Rosenthal and Richard Marshall.

Stockholm, Moderna Museet. *Jonathan Borofsky* (exhibition catalogue), 1984. Texts by Olle Granath, Joan Simon, Dieter Koepplin, and Richard Armstrong.

Alexander Calder

Arnason, H. H., with Alexander Calder and Ugo Mulas. *Calder*. New York: Viking Press, 1971.

Lipman, Jean, ed., with Nancy Foote. *Calder's Circus*. New York: E. P. Dutton and Co. for the Whitney Museum of American Art, 1972.

New York, The Museum of Modern Art. *Alexander Calder* (exhibition catalogue), 1951. Catalogue by James Johnson Sweeney.

New York, Whitney Museum of American Art. *Calder's Universe* (exhibition catalogue), 1976. Catalogue by Jean Lipman.

Turin, Italy, Palazzo a Vela. *Calder: Mostra Retrospettiva* (exhibition catalogue), 1983. Catalogue by Giovanni Carandente.

Charles Burchfield

Baur, John I. H. *Life and Work of Charles Burchfield 1893–1967: The Inlander*. Newark, Delaware: University of Delaware Press, 1982.

The Cleveland Museum of Art and the Print Club of Cleveland. *The Drawings of Charles Burchfield* (exhibition catalogue), 1953. Catalogue by Leona E. Prasse.

Jones, Edith H., ed. *The Drawings of Charles Burchfield*. New York: Praeger Publishers in association with The Drawing Society, 1968.

New York, Whitney Museum of American Art. *Charles Burchfield* (exhibition catalogue), 1956. Catalogue by John I. H. Baur.

————. *Charles Burchfield: A Concentration of Works from the Permanent Collection of the Whitney Museum of American Art* (exhibition catalogue), 1980. Catalogue by Patterson Sims.

Tucson, University of Arizona. *His Golden Year: A Retrospective Exhibition of Watercolors, Oils and Graphics by Charles E. Burchfield* (exhibition catalogue), 1965. Introduction by William E. Steadman, text by Charles Burchfield.

Utica, New York, Munson-Williams-Proctor Institute. *Charles Burchfield* (exhibition catalogue), 1970. Catalogue by Joseph S. Trovato.

Federico Castellon

Freundlich, August L. *Federico Castellon: His Graphic Works 1936–1971*. Syracuse, New York: College of Visual and Performing Arts, Syracuse University, 1978.

Christo

Alloway, Lawrence. *Christo*. New York: Harry N. Abrams, 1969.

Bourdon, David. *Christo*. New York: Harry N. Abrams, 1972.

Bourdon, David, and Calvin Tomkins. *Christo: Running Fence, Sonoma and Marin Counties, California 1972–76*. New York: Harry N. Abrams, 1978.

Spies, Werner. *The Running Fence Project: Christo*. New York: Harry N. Abrams, 1977.

Chuck Close

Austin, Texas, Laguna Gloria Art Museum. *Chuck Close: Dot Drawings 1973–1975* (exhibition catalogue), 1975. Catalogue by Christopher Finch.

La Jolla Museum of Contemporary Art, California, organized by the Daniel Weinberg Gallery, San Francisco. *Richard Artschwager, Chuck Close, Joe Zucker* (exhibition catalogue), 1976. Catalogue by Catherine Cord.

Minneapolis, Walker Art Center. *Close Portraits* (exhibition catalogue), 1980. Catalogue by Lisa Lyons and Martin Friedman.

Stuart Davis

Goossen, E. C. *Stuart Davis*. New York: George Braziller, 1959.

Kelder, Diane, ed. *Stuart Davis*. New York: Praeger Publishers, 1971.

New York, The Brooklyn Museum. *Stuart Davis: Art and Art Theory* (exhibition catalogue), 1978. Catalogue by John R. Lane.

New York, Whitney Museum of American Art. *Stuart Davis: A Concentration of Works from the Permanent Collection of the Whitney Museum of American Art* (exhibition catalogue), 1980. Catalogue by Patterson Sims.

Washington, D.C., National Collection of Fine Arts, Smithsonian Institution. *Stuart Davis Memorial Exhibition 1894–1964* (exhibition catalogue), 1965. Catalogue by H. H. Arnason.

Willem de Kooning

Minneapolis, Walker Art Center. *De Kooning: Drawings/Sculptures* (exhibition catalogue), 1974. Catalogue by Philip Larson and Peter Schjeldahl.

New York, The Museum of Modern Art. *Willem de Kooning* (exhibition catalogue), 1969. Catalogue by Thomas B. Hess.

New York, The Solomon R. Guggenheim Museum. *Willem de Kooning in East Hampton* (exhibition catalogue), 1978. Catalogue by Diane Waldman.

New York, Whitney Museum of American Art. *Willem de Kooning: Drawings, Paintings, Sculpture* (exhibition catalogue) 1983. Texts by Paul Cummings, Jörn Merkert, and Claire Stoullig.

Northampton, Massachusetts, Smith College Museum of Art. *Willem de Kooning: A Retrospective Exhibition from Public and Private Collections* (exhibition catalogue), 1965. Catalogue by Dore Ashton.

Rosenberg, Harold. *De Kooning.* New York: Harry N. Abrams, 1974.

Charles Demuth

Gallatin, A. E. *Charles Demuth.* New York: William Edward Rudge, 1927.

New York, The Museum of Modern Art. *Charles Demuth* (exhibition catalogue), 1950. Texts by Andrew Carnduff Ritchie and Marcel Duchamp.

New York, Whitney Museum of American Art. *Charles Demuth Memorial Exhibition* (exhibition catalogue), 1937. Text by Henry McBride.

Norton, Thomas E., ed. *Homage to Charles Demuth: Still Life Painter of Lancaster.* Ephrata, Pennsylvania: Science Press, 1978. Texts by Alvord L. Eiseman, Sherman E. Lee, and Gerald S. Lestz, valedictory by Marsden Hartley.

Edwin Dickinson

Buffalo, New York, State University of New York, College at Buffalo, Burchfield Center. *Edwin Dickinson: Tribute Exhibition* (exhibition catalogue), 1977. Texts by Edna M. Lindemann, Thomas W. Leavitt, and Frances Dickinson.

Goodrich, Lloyd. *The Drawings of Edwin Dickinson.* New York: The Drawing Society in association with Yale University Press, 1963.

New York, National Academy of Design. *Edwin Dickinson: Draftsman/Painter* (exhibition catalogue), 1982. Introduction by John H. Dobkin, text by John Ashbery, recollection by Elaine de Kooning.

New York, Whitney Museum of American Art. *Edwin Dickinson* (exhibition catalogue), 1965. Catalogue by Lloyd Goodrich.

Richard Diebenkorn

Buffalo, New York, Albright-Knox Art Gallery. *Richard Diebenkorn: Paintings and Drawings 1943–1976* (exhibition catalogue), 1976. Texts by Robert T. Buck, Jr., Linda L. Cathcart, Gerald Nordland, and Maurice Tuchman.

Pasadena Art Museum, California. *Richard Diebenkorn* (exhibition catalogue), 1960. Introduction by Thomas W. Leavitt.

Stanford University, Department of Art and Architecture, California. *Drawings by Richard Diebenkorn* (exhibition catalogue), 1965. Introduction by Lorenz Eitner.

Washington, D.C., Washington Gallery of Modern Art. *Richard Diebenkorn: A Retrospective Exhibition* (exhibition catalogue), 1964. Text by Gerald Nordland.

Burgoyne Diller

Minneapolis, Walker Art Center. *Burgoyne Diller* (exhibition catalogue), 1971. Catalogue by Philip Larson.

Arthur G. Dove

Cohn, Sherrye. *Arthur Dove: Nature as Symbol.* Ann Arbor, Michigan: UMI Research Press, 1985.

Ithaca, New York, Andrew Dickson White Museum of Art, Cornell University. *Arthur G. Dove, 1880–1946: A Retrospective Exhibition* (exhibition catalogue), 1954. Text by Alan Solomon.

Los Angeles, Art Galleries of the University of California, Los Angeles. *Arthur G. Dove* (exhibition catalogue), 1958. Catalogue by Frederick S. Wight.

Morgan, Ann Lee. *Arthur Dove: Life and Work, with a Catalogue Raisonné.* Newark, Delaware: University of Delaware Press, 1984.

San Francisco Museum of Art. *Arthur Dove* (exhibition catalogue), 1974. Catalogue by Barbara Haskell.

Rackstraw Downes

Hirschl & Adler Modern, New York. *Rackstraw Downes* (exhibition catalogue), 1984. Introduction by John Yau.

Arshile Gorky

Jordan, Jim M., and Robert Goldwater. *The Paintings of Arshile Gorky: A Critical Catalogue.* New York: New York University Press, 1980.

Joyner, Brooks. *The Drawings of Arshile Gorky.* College Park, Maryland: University of Maryland Press, 1969.

Levy, Julien. *Arshile Gorky.* New York: Harry N. Abrams, 1966.

New York, International Council of the Museum of Modern Art. *Arshile Gorky Drawings* (exhibition catalogue), 1962. Catalogue by Frank O'Hara.

New York, The Museum of Modern Art. *Arshile Gorky: Paintings, Drawings, Studies* (exhibition catalogue), 1962. Catalogue by William C. Seitz, foreword by Julien Levy.

New York, The Solomon R. Guggenheim Museum. *Arshile Gorky 1904–1948: A Retrospective* (exhibition catalogue), 1981. Catalogue by Diane Waldman.

New York, Whitney Museum of American Art. *Arshile Gorky Memorial Exhibition* (exhibition catalogue), 1951. Text by Ethel K. Schwabacher, biographical notes by Lloyd Goodrich.

Oklahoma City, Oklahoma Art Center. *An Exhibition of Drawings by Arshile Gorky* (exhibition catalogue), 1973. Text by Karlen Mooradian.

Schwabacher, Ethel K. *Arshile Gorky.* New York: Macmillan Co. for the Whitney Museum of American Art, 1957.

Morris Graves

Cage, John. *The Drawings of Morris Graves with Comments by the Artist.* Boston: New York Graphic Society for The Drawing Society, 1974.

Eugene, Oregon, University of Oregon Museum of Art. *Morris Graves: A Retrospective* (exhibition catalogue), 1966. Texts by Nancy Wilson Ross, Virginia Haseltine, and Gerald Heard, statements by Morris Graves.

Los Angeles, Art Galleries of the University of California, Los Angeles. *Morris Graves* (exhibition catalogue), 1956. Introduction by John I. H. Baur, texts by Frederick S. Wight and Duncan Phillips.

Washington, D.C., The Phillips Collection. *Morris Graves: Vision of the Inner Eye* (exhibition catalogue), 1983. Catalogue by Ray Kass, texts by Duncan Phillips, Theodore F. Wolff, and Marsden Hartley.

Philip Guston

Ashton, Dore. *Philip Guston.* New York: Grove Press, 1960.

————. *A Critical Study of Philip Guston: Yes, But . . .* New York: Viking Press, 1976.

London, Whitechapel Art Gallery. *Philip Guston: Paintings 1969–80* (exhibition catalogue), 1982. Texts by Norbert Lynton and Philip Guston.

New York, The Jewish Museum. *Philip Guston: Recent Paintings and Drawings* (exhibition catalogue), 1966. Catalogue by Sam Hunter.

New York, The Solomon R. Guggenheim Museum. *Philip Guston* (exhibition catalogue), 1962. Catalogue by H. H. Arnason.

San Francisco Museum of Modern Art. *Philip Guston* (exhibition catalogue), 1980. Texts by Ross Feld and Henry T. Hopkins, statement by Philip Guston.

Marsden Hartley

Hartley, Marsden. *Adventures in the Arts.* New York: Boni and Liveright, 1921.

Hartley, Marsden, edited by Gail R. Scott. *On Art.* New York: Horizon Press, 1982.

McCausland, Elizabeth. *Marsden Hartley.* Minneapolis: University of Minnesota Press, 1952.

New York, Whitney Museum of American Art. *Marsden Hartley* (exhibition catalogue), 1980. Catalogue by Barbara Haskell.

Washington, D.C., Smithsonian Institution Traveling Exhibition Service. *Ninety-nine Drawings by Marsden Hartley* (exhibition catalogue), 1970. Catalogue by William J. Mitchell.

Michael Heizer

The Detroit Institute of Arts. *Michael Heizer / Actual Size* (exhibition catalogue), 1971.

Essen, West Germany, Museum Folkwang, and Rijksmuseum Kröller-Müller, Otterlo, The Netherlands. *Michael Heizer* (exhibition catalogue), 1979. Texts by Michael Heizer, Zdenek Felix, and Ellen Joosten.

Los Angeles, The Museum of Contemporary Art. *Michael Heizer: Sculpture in Reverse* (exhibition catalogue), 1984. Edited by Julia Brown, compiled in collaboration with Barbara Heizer.

Al Held

San Francisco Museum of Art. *Al Held* (exhibition catalogue), 1968. Text by Eleanor Green.

New York, Whitney Museum of American Art. *Al Held* (exhibition catalogue), 1974. Catalogue by Marcia Tucker.

Edward Hopper

Goodrich, Lloyd. *Edward Hopper.* New York: Harry N. Abrams, 1971.

Levin, Gail. *Edward Hopper: The Art and the Artist.* New York: W. W. Norton & Co. in association with the Whitney Museum of American Art, 1980.

New York, The Museum of Modern Art. *Edward Hopper: Retrospective Exhibition* (exhibition catalogue), 1933. Catalogue by Alfred H. Barr, Jr.

New York, Whitney Museum of American Art. *Edward Hopper: Exhibition and Catalogue* (exhibition catalogue), 1964. Catalogue by Lloyd Goodrich.

_____. *Edward Hopper: Selections from the Hopper Bequest* (exhibition catalogue), 1971. Catalogue by Lloyd Goodrich.

Earle Horter

The Philadelphia Art Alliance. *Earle Horter: Watercolors, Oils, Drawings, Prints* (exhibition catalogue), 1954. Catalogue by Henry C. Pitz.

Richard Hunt

New York, The Museum of Modern Art. *The Sculpture of Richard Hunt* (exhibition catalogue), 1971. Catalogue by William S. Lieberman.

Bill Jensen

New York, The Museum of Modern Art. *Bill Jensen: First Etchings* (exhibition catalogue), 1986. Catalogue by Deborah Wye.

Jasper Johns

Kosloff, Max. *Jasper Johns* (Meridian Modern Artists). New York: Harry N. Abrams, 1974.

London, Arts Council of Great Britain. *Jasper Johns Drawings* (exhibition catalogue), 1974. Interview by David Sylvester.

London, Whitechapel Art Gallery. *Jasper Johns: Paintings, Drawings and Sculpture 1954–1964* (exhibition catalogue), 1964. Catalogue by Alan R. Solomon.

New York, The Jewish Museum. *Jasper Johns* (exhibition catalogue), 1964. Catalogue by Alan R. Solomon.

New York, The Museum of Modern Art. *Jasper Johns: A Print Retrospective* (exhibition catalogue), 1986. Catalogue by Riva Castleman.

New York, Whitney Museum of American Art. *Jasper Johns* (exhibition catalogue), 1977. Catalogue by Michael Crichton.

Paris, Musée National d'Art Moderne, Centre Georges Pompidou. *Jasper Johns* (exhibition catalogue), 1978. Texts by Pontus Hulten, Alain Robbe-Grillet and Pierre Restany.

Shapiro, David. *Jasper Johns Drawings 1954–1984.* New York: Harry N. Abrams, 1984.

Steinberg, Leo. "Jasper Johns: The First Seven Years of His Art" (1962). In *Other Criteria: Confrontations with Twentieth-Century Art.* New York: Oxford University Press, 1972.

Ellsworth Kelly

Amsterdam, Stedelijk Museum. *Ellsworth Kelly: Paintings and Sculptures: 1963–1979* (exhibition catalogue), 1979. Catalogue by Barbara Rose.

Coplans, John. *Ellsworth Kelly.* New York: Harry N. Abrams, 1971.

New York, The Museum of Modern Art. *Ellsworth Kelly* (exhibition catalogue), 1973. Catalogue by E. C. Goossen.

New York, Whitney Museum of American Art. *Ellsworth Kelly: Sculpture* (exhibition catalogue), 1982. Catalogue by Patterson Sims and Emily Rauh Pulitzer.

Waldman, Diane. *Ellsworth Kelly: Drawings, Collages, Prints.* Greenwich, Connecticut: New York Graphic Society, 1971

Washington, D.C., Washington Gallery of Modern Art. *Paintings, Sculpture and Drawings by Ellsworth Kelly* (exhibition catalogue), 1963. Foreword by Adelyn D. Breeskin, interview by Henry Geldzahler.

Franz Kline

Dawson, Fielding. *An Emotional Memoir of Franz Kline.* New York: Pantheon Books, 1967.

London, Whitechapel Art Gallery. *Franz Kline* (exhibition catalogue), 1964. Catalogue by Frank O'Hara.

New York, Whitney Museum of American Art. *Franz Kline 1910–1962* (exhibition catalogue), 1968. Catalogue by John Gordon.

Washington, D.C., The Phillips Collection. *Franz Kline: The Color Abstractions* (exhibition catalogue), 1979. Text by Robert Motherwell.

Washington, D.C., Washington Gallery of Modern Art. *Franz Kline: Memorial Exhibition* (exhibition catalogue), 1962. Catalogue by Elaine de Kooning.

Yasuo Kuniyoshi

Gainesville, Florida, University Gallery, University of Florida. *Yasuo Kuniyoshi* (exhibition catalogue), 1969. Catalogue by Roy C. Craven and Lloyd Goodrich.

New York, Whitney Museum of American Art. *Kuniyoshi* (exhibition catalogue), 1948. Catalogue by Lloyd Goodrich.

Tokyo, National Museum of Modern Art. *Kuniyoshi* (exhibition catalogue), 1954. Catalogue by Lloyd Goodrich and Asuo Imaizumi.

Roy Lichtenstein

Alloway, Lawrence. *Roy Lichtenstein* (Modern Masters Series). New York: Abbeville Press, 1983.

Bern, Switzerland, Kunsthalle Bern. *Roy Lichtenstein* (exhibition catalogue), 1968. Catalogue by Jean-Christophe Ammann and W. A. L. Beeren.

Coplans, John, ed. *Roy Lichtenstein* (Documentary Monographs in Modern Art). New York: Praeger Publishers, 1972.

Houston, Contemporary Arts Museum. *Roy Lichtenstein* (exhibition catalogue), 1972. Catalogue by Lawrence Alloway.

London, The Tate Gallery. *Roy Lichtenstein* (exhibition catalogue), 1968. Catalogue by Richard Morphet.

New York, James Goodman Gallery. *Roy Lichtenstein: A Drawing Retrospective* (exhibition catalogue), 1984. Catalogue by Robert-Pincus Witten.

New York, The Solomon R. Guggenheim Museum. *Roy Lichtenstein* (exhibition catalogue), 1969. Catalogue by Diane Waldman.

Pasadena Art Museum, California, in collaboration with the Walker Art Center, Minneapolis. *Roy Lichtenstein* (exhibition catalogue), 1967. Catalogue by John Coplans.

Richard Lindner

Ashton, Dore. *Richard Lindner.* New York: Harry N. Abrams, 1969.

Berkeley, University Art Museum, University of California. *Lindner* (exhibition catalogue), 1969. Text by Dore Ashton.

Chicago, Museum of Contemporary Art. *Richard Lindner: A Retrospective Exhibition* (exhibition catalogue), 1977. Interview by Stephen Prokopoff.

Dienst, Rolf-Gunter. *Richard Lindner.* New York: Harry N. Abrams, 1970.

Kramer, Hilton. *Richard Linder.* Boston: New York Graphic Society, 1975.

Paris, Musée National d'Art Moderne. *Richard Lindner* (exhibition catalogue), 1974. Catalogue by Jean-Hubert Martin.

Tillim, Sidney. *Richard Lindner.* Chicago: William and Noma Copley Foundation, 1960.

Louis Lozowick

Long Beach Museum of Art, California. *Louis Lozowick, American Precisionist: Retrospective* (exhibition catalogue), 1978. Catalogue by John Bowlt.

Reginald Marsh

Goodrich, Lloyd. *Reginald Marsh.* New York: Harry N. Abrams, 1972.

Laning, Edward. *The Sketchbooks of Reginald Marsh.* Greenwich, Connecticut: New York Graphic Society, 1973.

Newport Beach, California, Newport Harbor Art Museum. *Reginald Marsh: A Retrospective Exhibition* (exhibition catalogue), 1972. Introduction by Thomas H. Garver.

New York, Whitney Museum of American Art. *Reginald Marsh* (exhibition catalogue), 1955. Catalogue by Lloyd Goodrich.

_____. *Reginald Marsh's New York: Paintings, Drawings, Prints and Photographs* (exhibition catalogue), 1983. Catalogue by Marilyn Cohen.

Walter Murch

Geneva, Galerie Jan Krugier. *Walter Murch* (exhibition catalogue), 1976. Catalogue by Paul Cummings.

Greenvale, New York, Hillwood Art Gallery, Long Island University, C. W. Post Campus. *Walter Murch: Paintings and Drawings* (exhibition catalogue), 1986. Catalogue by Judy Collischan Van Wagner, texts by Van Wagner, Paul Cummings, and Daniel Robbins.

Providence, Rhode Island School of Design. *Walter Murch* (exhibition catalogue), 1966. Catalogue by Daniel Robbins.

Elizabeth Murray

Pittsburgh, Carnegie-Mellon University Art Gallery. *Elizabeth Murray: Drawings: 1980–1986* (exhibition catalogue), 1986. Catalogue by Elaine A. King.

Elie Nadelman

Kirstein, Lincoln. *Elie Nadelman.* New York: Eakins Press, 1973.

_____. *Elie Nadelman Drawings.* New York: H. Bittner and Co., 1949.

New York, The Museum of Modern Art. *The Sculpture of Elie Nadelman* (exhibition catalogue), 1948. Catalogue by Lincoln Kirstein.

New York, Whitney Museum of American Art. *The Sculpture and Drawings of Elie Nadelman* (exhibition catalogue), 1975. Catalogue by John I. H. Baur.

Jim Nutt

Chicago, Museum of Contemporary Art. *Jim Nutt* (exhibition catalogue), 1974. Catalogue by Whitney Halstead.

Georgia O'Keeffe

Castro, Jan Garden. *The Art and Life of Georgia O'Keeffe.* New York: Crown Publishers, 1985.

Fort Worth, Amon Carter Museum of Western Art. *Georgia O'Keeffe: An Exhibition of the Work of the Artist from 1915–1966* (exhibition catalogue), 1966. Edited by Mitchell A. Wilder.

New York, Whitney Museum of American Art. *Georgia O'Keeffe* (exhibition catalogue), 1970. Catalogue by Lloyd Goodrich and Doris Bry.

O'Keeffe, Georgia. *A Studio Book.* New York: Viking Press, 1976.

Worcester Art Museum, Massachusetts. *Georgia O'Keeffe* (exhibition catalogue), 1960. Catalogue by Daniel Catton Rich.

Claes Oldenburg

Baro, Gene. *Claes Oldenburg, Drawings and Prints.* New York: Chelsea House Publishers, 1969.

Johnson, Ellen H. *Claes Oldenburg.* Baltimore: Penguin Books, 1971.

Minneapolis, Walker Art Center. *Oldenburg: Six Themes* (exhibition catalogue), 1975. Catalogue by Claes Oldenburg.

New York, The Museum of Modern Art. *Claes Oldenburg* (exhibition catalogue), 1969. Catalogue by Barbara Rose.

Paris, Musée National d'Art Moderne, Centre Georges Pompidou. *Claes Oldenburg: Dessins, Aquarelles et Estampes* (exhibition catalogue), 1977. Catalogue by Coosje van Bruggen.

Tübingen, West Germany, Kunsthalle Tübingen. *Zeichnungen von Claes Oldenburg* (exhibition catalogue), 1975. Catalogue by Götz Adriani, Dieter Koepplin, and Barbara Rose.

Van Bruggen, Coosje, and Claes Oldenburg. *Claes Oldenburg: Large-Scale Projects 1977–1980.* New York: Rizzoli International Publications, 1980.

Alfonso Ossorio

Friedman, B. H. *Alfonso Ossorio.* New York: Harry N. Abrams, 1971.

Tapie, Michel. *Ossorio.* Turin, Italy: Edizioni d'Arte Fratelli Pozzo, 1961.

Jackson Pollock

Düsseldorf, Städtische Kunsthalle Düsseldorf. *Jackson Pollock: Drawing into Painting* (exhibition catalogue), 1979. Text by Bernice Rose.

New York, The Museum of Modern Art in association with The Drawing Society. *Jackson Pollock* (exhibition catalogue), 1956. Catalogue by Sam Hunter.

————. *Jackson Pollock: Works on Paper* (exhibition catalogue), 1969. Catalogue by Bernice Rose.

O'Connor, Francis Valentine, edited by Eugene Victor Thaw. *Jackson Pollock: A Catalogue Raisonné of Paintings, Drawings, and Other Works.* 4 vols. New Haven: Yale University Press, 1978.

O'Hara, Frank. *Jackson Pollock.* New York: Georgie Braziller, 1959.

Paris, Musée National d'Art Moderne, Centre Georges Pompidou. *Jackson Pollock* (exhibition catalogue), 1982. Texts by William Rubin, Barbara Rose, and others.

Robertson, Bryan. *Jackson Pollock.* New York: Harry N. Abrams, 1960.

Maurice Prendergast

Boston, Museum of Fine Arts. *Maurice Prendergast, 1859–1924* (exhibition catalogue), 1960. Catalogue by Hedley Howell Rhys.

College Park, Maryland, University of Maryland Art Gallery. *Maurice Prendergast: Art of Impulse and Color* (exhibition catalogue), 1976. Catalogue by Eleanor Green and Jeffrey R. Hayes.

New York, Whitney Museum of American Art. *Maurice B. Prendergast: A Concentration of Works from the Permanent Collection* (exhibition catalogue), 1980. Catalogue by Patterson Sims.

Scott, David W. *Maurice Prendergast.* Washington, D.C.: The Phillips Collection, 1980.

Robert Rauschenberg

Adriani, Götz. *Robert Rauschenberg: Zeichnungen, Gouachen, Collagen, 1949 bis 1979.* Munich: R. Piper Verlag, 1982.

Berlin, Staatliche Kunsthalle Berlin. *Robert Rauschenberg: Werke 1950–1980* (exhibition catalogue), 1980. Texts by Lawrence Alloway, Götz Adriani, and William S. Lieberman.

Forge, Andrew. *Robert Rauschenberg.* New York: Harry N. Abrams, 1969.

————. *Robert Rauschenberg.* New York: Harry N. Abrams, 1972.

London, Whitechapel Art Gallery. *Robert Rauschenberg: Paintings, Drawings and Combines, 1949–1964* (exhibition catalogue), 1964. Texts by Henry Geldzahler, John Cage, and Max Kozloff.

New York, Acquavella Contemporary Art. *Robert Rauschenberg Drawings: 1958–1968* (exhibition catalogue), 1986. Catalogue by Lawrence Alloway.

New York, The Jewish Museum. *Robert Rauschenberg* (exhibition catalogue), 1963. Catalogue by Alan R. Solomon.

Washington, D.C., National Collection of Fine Arts, Smithsonian Institution. *Robert Rauschenberg* (exhibition catalogue), 1976. Catalogue by Daniel Robbins, text by Lawrence Alloway.

Ad Reinhardt

Lippard, Lucy R. *Ad Reinhardt*. New York: Harry N. Abrams, 1981.

New York, The Jewish Museum. *Ad Reinhardt* (exhibition catalogue), 1967. Catalogue by Lucy R. Lippard, preface by Sam Hunter.

Rose, Barbara, ed. *Art as Art: The Selected Writings of Ad Reinhardt*. New York: Viking Press, 1975.

Stuttgart, Staatsgalerie Stuttgart. *Ad Reinhardt* (exhibition catalogue), 1985. Catalogue by Gudrun Inboden and Thomas Kellein.

James Rosenquist

Goldman, Judith. *James Rosenquist*. New York: Viking Penguin, 1985.

New York, Whitney Museum of American Art. *James Rosenquist* (exhibition catalogue), 1972. Catalogue by Marcia Tucker.

Sarasota, Florida, John and Mable Ringling Museum of Art. *James Rosenquist Graphics Retrospective* (exhibition catalogue), 1979. Catalogue by Elayne H. Varian.

Theodore Roszak

Chicago, The Art Institute of Chicago. *In Pursuit of an Image* (exhibition catalogue), 1955. Catalogue by Theodore Roszak.

Fort Lauderdale, Museum of Art. *Theodore Roszak: Recent Drawings* (exhibition catalogue), 1981. Catalogue by George S. Bolge.

Minneapolis, Walker Art Center. *Theodore Roszak* (exhibition catalogue), 1956. Catalogue by H. H. Arnason.

Edward Ruscha

Auckland City Art Gallery, New Zealand. *Graphic Works by Edward Ruscha* (exhibition catalogue), 1978. Catalogue by Henry Geldzahler and Andrew Bogle.

Buffalo, New York, Albright-Knox Art Gallery. *Edward Ruscha* (exhibition catalogue), 1976. Catalogue by Linda L. Cathcart.

Minneapolis Institute of Arts. *Edward Ruscha/(Ed-Werd Ray-Shay) Young Artist* (exhibition catalogue), 1972.

Ruscha, Edward. *Guacamole Airlines and Other Drawings*. New York: Harry N. Abrams, 1976.

San Francisco Museum of Modern Art. *The Works of Edward Ruscha* (exhibition catalogue), 1982. Foreword by Henry T. Hopkins, introduction by Anne Livet, texts by Dave Hickey and Peter Plagens.

Kay Sage

Ithaca, New York, Herbert F. Johnson Museum of Art, Cornell University. *Kay Sage* (exhibition catalogue), 1977. Catalogue by Regine Tessier Krieger.

New York, Catherine Viviano Gallery. *Kay Sage Retrospective* (exhibition catalogue), 1960. Catalogue by James Thrall Soby.

Lucas Samaras

Chicago, Museum of Contemporary Art. *Lucas Samaras: Boxes* (exhibition catalogue), 1971. Text by Joan C. Siegfried.

Levin, Kim. *Lucas Samaras*. New York: Harry N. Abrams, 1975.

New York, Whitney Museum of American Art. *Lucas Samaras* (exhibition catalogue), 1973. Catalogue by Lucas Samaras and Robert Doty.

Samaras, Lucas. *Samaras Album: Autointerview, Autobiography, Autopolaroid*. New York: Whitney Museum of American Art and Pace Editions, 1971.

Charles Sheeler

Cambridge, Massachusetts, The New Gallery, Charles Hayden Memorial Library, Massachusetts Institute of Technology. *Charles Sheeler* (exhibition catalogue), 1959.

Friedman, Martin. *Charles Sheeler*. New York: Watson-Guptill Publications, 1975.

Los Angeles, Art Galleries of the University of California, Los Angeles. *Charles Sheeler: A Retrospective Exhibition* (exhibition catalogue), 1954. Foreword by William Carlos Williams, texts by Bartlett H. Hayes, Jr. and Frederick S. Wight.

New York, The Museum of Modern Art. *Charles Sheeler* (exhibition catalogue), 1939. Catalogue by William Carlos Williams.

University Park, Pennsylvania, Pennsylvania State University. *Charles Sheeler: The Works on Paper* (exhibition catalogue), 1974. Catalogue by John P. Driscoll.

Washington, D.C., National Collection of Fine Arts, Smithsonian Institution. *Charles Sheeler* (exhibition catalogue), 1968. Texts by Martin Friedman, Bartlett Hayes, and Charles Millard.

David Smith

Cambridge, Massachusetts, Fogg Art Museum, Harvard University. *David Smith 1906–1965: A Retrospective Exhibition* (exhibition catalogue), 1966. Catalogue by Jane Harrison Cone.

Clark, Trinkett. *The Drawings of David Smith*. New York: The Arts Publisher for the International Exhibitions Foundation, 1985.

Düsseldorf, Kunstsammlung Nordrhein-Westfalen. *David Smith: Skulpturen, Zeichnungen* (exhibition catalogue), 1986. Texts by Jörn Merkert, Hannelore Kersting, and Rachel Kirby.

Los Angeles County Museum of Art. *David Smith: A Memorial Exhibition* (exhibition catalogue), 1965. Catalogue by Hilton Kramer.

Marcus, Stanley E. *David Smith: The Sculptor and His Work*. Ithaca, New York: Cornell University Press, 1983.

McCoy, Garnett, ed. *David Smith*. New York: Praeger Publishers 1973.

New York, The Solomon R. Guggenheim Museum. *David Smith* (exhibition catalogue), 1969. Catalogue by Edward Fry.

New York, Whitney Museum of American Art. *David Smith: The Drawings* (exhibition catalogue), 1979. Catalogue by Paul Cummings.

Smith, David. *David Smith*. New York: Holt, Rinehart and Winston, 1968.

Wilkin, Karen. *David Smith*. New York: Abbeville Press, 1984.

Joseph Stella

Baur, John I. H. *Joseph Stella*. New York: Praeger Publishers, 1971.

Jaffe, Irma B. *Joseph Stella*. Cambridge: Harvard University Press, 1970.

The Newark Museum, New Jersey. *Joseph Stella: A Retrospective Exhibition* (exhibition catalogue), 1939. Preface by Arthur F. Egner.

New York, Whitney Museum of American Art. *Joseph Stella* (exhibition catalogue), 1963. Catalogue by John I. H. Baur.

Cy Twombly

Bastian, Heiner. *Cy Twombly: Zeichnungen 1953–1973*. Frankfurt: Verlag Ullstein; Berlin: Propyläen Verlag, 1973.

_____. *Cy Twombly: Bilder Paintings 1952–1976*. vol. 1. Frankfurt: Verlag Ullstein, 1978.

Bern, Switzerland, Kunsthalle Bern. *Cy Twombly: Bilder 1953–1972* (exhibition catalogue), 1973. Text by Michael Petzet.

New York, Whitney Museum of American Art. *Cy Twombly: Paintings and Drawings 1954–1977* (exhibition catalogue), 1979. Catalogue by David Whitney.

Philadelphia, Institute of Contemporary Art, University of Pennsylvania. *Cy Twombly: Paintings, Drawings, Constructions 1951–1974* (exhibition catalogue), 1975. Catalogue by Suzanne Delehanty and Heiner Bastian.

H. C. Westermann

Los Angeles County Museum of Art. *H. C. Westermann* (exhibition catalogue), 1968. Catalogue by Max Kozloff.

New York, Whitney Museum of American Art. *H. C. Westermann* (exhibition catalogue), 1978. Catalogue by Barbara Haskell.

John Wilde

Madison, Wisconsin, Elvehjem Museum of Art, University of Wisconsin. *John Wilde: Drawings 1940–1984* (exhibition catalogue), 1984. Catalogue by Carlton Overland.

William T. Wiley

Berkeley, University Art Museum, University of California. *William T. Wiley* (exhibition catalogue), 1971. Catalogue by Brenda Richardson.

Minneapolis, Walker Art Center. *Wiley Territory* (exhibition catalogue), 1979. Catalogue by Graham W. J. Beal and John Perreault.

Grant Wood

Dennis, James M. *Grant Wood: A Study in American Art and Culture*. New York: Viking Press, 1975.

Liffring-Zug, Joan, ed. *This Is Grant Wood Country*. Davenport, Iowa: Davenport Municipal Art Gallery, 1977.

The Minneapolis Institute of Arts. *Grant Wood: The Regionalist Vision* (exhibition catalogue), 1983. Catalogue by Wanda M. Corn.